The Spirits of Shoemakersville Road

JEFFREY A. DENGLER

Dedication

I dedicate this book to my ancestors. I honor you in my daily life. You had struggles, sacrifices, and trauma, but you also had love, hope, resilience, and the strength to overcome it all. Any hardships I go through in life I know and feel your spirit with me, guiding me. Because of you I have a solid foundation.

Our Ancestors are an ever widening circle of hope.
—Toni Morrison

We are all ghosts. We all carry, inside us, people who came before us.
—Liam Callanan

Table of Contents

Introduction

I always want to hear someone's beliefs. Even though I may not be in line with them, I keep an open mind. It always amazes me how many beliefs are out there. Who is right? How can one person or group of people be right and everyone else is wrong? What forms someone's belief system? What happened in their life that gave them their perception? Is it an inner knowing? Is it the cause of their surroundings and what they were taught? Is it a little of both? What forms our beliefs, our perception, our reality?

I had never been a religious person. I went to Sunday school as a child, went to service on and off as I became an adult, but never on a consistent basis. Even as a child, I knew within that I believed in God, Jesus, Angels, life after death. I always felt deep down there was something more, something greater than us. I never felt comfortable inside a church. I always felt God is in us, a part of us, around us. All we had to do was open our eyes to truly see. I felt I didn't have to dress up, go to church, and be around a lot of people to show I believed. I could worship my own way. It all just felt phony to me.

It felt like everyone was playing a part, being nice and acting a certain way in the church, but once they were in their normal life, they were everything but what they wanted everyone to perceive while in church.

I also couldn't understand how or why there were hundreds of religions out there. Again, how could only one be correct? One thing that was a constant in all religions was love. That one word connects all of them and all of us, in my opinion. Love is the constant. I feel it doesn't matter what path of light you take because they all lead to the same destination in the end.

Later in life, I experienced a traumatic event. This event opened me up to an awakening and an expansion of my beliefs. Those core beliefs didn't change, but more like validated to me how I always had that inner knowing. I not only felt, but now the other side shows me things that make me in awe of spirit and very humbled by it.

These experiences have changed me. I know without a doubt there is something greater than us. Angels are real. We may physically die, but our spirit, our soul lives on. Our loved ones are always with us. We need them and they are there by our side. It is extremely hard and traumatic losing a loved one. They do not want us being sad and depressed over them. They want us to live our life and be happy. Many times they send signs to let us know they are with us still and that we are never truly alone.

This story you are about to read is the true account of a very special case that will always be in my mind and heart. All of what I said above comes into play. The story surrounds an eighty-four-year-old woman by the name of Mary Lou. Many years ago as teenagers, I got to know her son, Todd. Even though I knew Todd since then, we never hung out, so sadly I didn't meet his mother until he asked me to come to his house due to the strange activity that was taking place.

During a span of about six weeks, so many things happened, including trusting in my own gifts/abilities, being in awe of spirit, humbled by spirit, question/ be mad at spirit, and in the end, have faith that what happens is meant to be and at times we have no control in an outcome. We aren't meant to know everything. There is a reason why we aren't told everything and we must have trust and faith in spirit and in the divine.

I call it "my gifts" because I truly believe these abilities are a gift from God. These abilities come to me in a few different ways. One is as a vision that plays out in midair right in front of me. A video will play out in midair, showing an event that usually then takes place within days. Another way is by closing my eyes and putting out an intention. I will see, hear, and feel things from the spirit world. When I am at a haunted location, I rarely see spirit. I feel and hear more than see. For some reason, I see more after I leave a location than I do while there. Once I get home and close my eyes, it is then that the images flash through my mind. The cause of this may be a form of protection, but maybe one day spirit will show themselves more readily.

During this process, I stopped second-guessing myself and put my trust in spirit and trust in the messages I receive. I also got to appreciate the opportunity to get to know a special person whose personality will stay with me.

I hope you enjoy this story and feel the roller coaster of emotions that were part of this case. It truly is a story of spirit in so many ways.

Chapter 1

Adventure Begins

March 5, 2018, I was talking to a friend named Todd who I knew since we were teenagers. Over the years, we ran into each other at work and usually the conversations were about news of old classmates and things that may have changed in their lives. The topic of the paranormal never came up. This one day, that all changed. We ran into each other and somehow got onto the subject of spirits.

When these conversations happen, I know it's for a reason and it has been guided to happen. I told him a few stories, and he said he believed me, could relate, and then went on to tell me a few times he experienced the paranormal.

It was about a week later and Todd stopped me. He said, "We talked about the paranormal last week and I now have a few things I want to tell you." He began to tell me about all the activity that had been happening lately in his home.

Todd said, "My daughter, Tina, was in the kitchen eating and I was in the dining room at the desk. I heard the back door open and then the garage open. Tina heard it and I heard it, but the thing is, Tina didn't say anything when it happened. I got up and went into the kitchen to question her. I asked her if someone came in because I heard the doors. Tina told me a guy came in the back door and then went into the attached garage. She wasn't scared or anything. I immediately went out to the garage and didn't see anything. I went down into the basement and didn't see anything. I came up the steps and nothing. It couldn't have been a real person. They couldn't have got out without me seeing them."

Todd continued with another story where Tina did get scared while she was in the basement. He said, "She would be down there, doing arts and crafts and would feel like someone was watching her. She would come upstairs to get me and when I would go down, nothing would be there."

He asked, "Would you like to come over to see if you can figure out what is going on and why it is happening?"

I told him, "Yeah, I will gladly help and if needed, one of our Medium friends could come over and conduct a walkthrough. Between us and the Medium, we will do our best to get you answers to why it is happening."

Todd said, "My parents bought the property and then built the home I live in now back in 1968. They raised three sons and one daughter in the home. I had another sister, but she died when she was a baby. My father passed away in the home in 1992. I bought the home from my mom in 1995. My mother, Mary Lou, lives in the home with me and my ten-year-old daughter, Christina, who goes by the name of Tina, and our dog, Coco."

I told Todd, "Talk it over with your family and let me know when is the best time for my wife and I to come over to talk to everyone and conduct a short investigation."

The next day, Todd informed me that the following Monday would be a good day to stop by.

In the meantime, I sent a photo of the front of the home to a Medium I knew. This particular Medium we will call Claire for this story. I send a photograph because everything holds energy, even pictures. Most, if not all, "gifted" people could look at a photo and feel the energy from it. The photo could be of a home, object, face, or anything, really. If it was a person, it was best for me and many others to be able to see their eyes. The eyes told the story and definitely were the windows to the soul.

Claire said she felt right away that there was spirit activity in the home and the first energy she felt was a male. She said she got a man's name, Paul, and he was with a woman that lived in the home. She mentioned another male spirit that felt to her like family. She felt there were many spirits involved and would be able to tell me more once she was at the home.

The following day, I conveyed to Todd what she had said. Todd felt the one male spirit was probably his dad, but the other one makes no sense. He said, "We don't know anyone named Paul who would be connected to us."

I told him, "Many times, even though it doesn't make sense now, more than likely, it will at a later date."

He shook his head and had a look on his face that told me it didn't matter how long in the future he waited, the name Paul would still not make any sense.

Within days, I had visions of what I felt was his property.

When I say visions, I see an event that plays out in front of me or I see it play out when I close my eyes. If these visions happen when my eyes are open, they just appear out of nowhere. It's like watching a video play in midair a few feet from me. When my eyes are closed, I see it in my mind's eye. One way to describe it is if you ever watched a show called *Stranger Things*. There is a character in this show by the name of Eleven. How this character has visions is very close to how it happens with me. In this particular vision, I saw a home that wasn't Todd's, but felt it was on his property at one time. It was dark brown or black, one floor with an overhang in front with a porch. The first description that came to mind when I saw it was a shanty or shack.

The remains of this structure resemble the shack I saw in a vision

A few days later, I had another vision. It looked to be the front yard of Todd's home, but the home was not part of the vision, just the yard. Another difference was there were a few steps that went down at the very front of the yard. My point of view was from standing at the right of these steps, looking at where the house should be.

Looking at an angle across the lawn about twenty yards away, a man was walking. He was slightly hunched over, balding, wearing wire-frame glasses. His right arm was bent, and in his hand he held a lantern. The lantern was about eye level. I watched him walk across the grass from right to left. As he walked, he turned his head to the left while the lantern and the rest of his body stayed the same. He turned his head, looked right at me, and smiled. It was a very friendly smile. After he smiled, he faded away. Immediately after this vision, I saw the same man again, but he was on the right side of the steps while I stood in the same area on the left. He was holding the lantern and on his right were three children. Looked to me like there were two girls and a boy. It was a dusk setting, and the children wore what looked like pajamas or a long, oversized nightshirt. They stood there for about five to seven seconds and then just faded away. I questioned Todd each time if any of this made sense, but every time Todd would say that nothing at all made sense.

Sketch of the man I saw in a vision.

Sketch of the three children and the
man I saw in in a vision.

"Well, it doesn't make sense at this time, but later it will all come together. It always does," I told him.

Chapter 2

Meet the Family

Monday March 26, 2018, about three forty-five p.m. we arrived at the home. The home is on a slight incline compared to Shoemakersville Road. The house sits back approximately forty to fifty yards from the road. We had driven up the driveway and parked in front of the attached two-car garage. The home has light tan, almost light yellowish colored siding. There are three windows side by side on the second floor, just about the same width as the porch roof. The porch roof and the house roof have matching brown shingles. The shutters on the sides of each window are also brown to match the shingles. The driveway and garage are located to the right side of the home. We walked up the driveway to the few steps that led to the raised concrete porch. We walked across the porch to the front door. After being greeted by Todd at the door, we entered and met his mom and his daughter.

There is a wooden main door and a wooden screen door. The screen door was a homemade one, painted red. It reminded me of one when I was a kid at my grandmother's house, the ones that you could hear the spring as you open it and then when you let it go, it slams. After the slam, I would hear my grandmother yell, "Stop slamming the door!"

All the kids would slam the door and would continue to do so every time, even though we would get yelled at. This time, though, I held the door so it wouldn't slam. My grandmother would be proud.

We entered the front door, and we were greeted by Todd's daughter, Tina, and their little dog, Coco. His mother was in her room, which was directly on the left after entering the front door. She was sitting on the far side of the room with her back to us. Todd yelled to her and when she turned, we could see that she was crocheting. She put her crocheting project down and came out to meet us. His mom's name was Mary Lou.

Todd told her, "They are here to try and figure out why we are having so much activity."

After Todd introduced us and told her why we were here, I said to Mary Lou, "We want to do a quick investigation to see if we can capture any evidence of spirits in the house to back up what is being experienced."

Tami asked Mary Lou, "Did anything happen to you in the house?"

Mary Lou said, "Yes." She began to tell us about her experiences. She pointed to her room and said, "When I sleep, I am awakened by what feels like someone lifting my arm and letting it go. I feel it could be my husband, Donald, that passed."

I looked at Todd because originally he felt it was his dad, too. I asked him, "Where in the house is the most activity?"

Todd said, "In the basement."

I asked, "Can we go into the basement and ask a few questions?"

Todd turned to his mom and explained to her that we were going into the basement and would be back upstairs after we were done. It shouldn't take too long. He explained this because his mom could not go up and down stairs due to her being eighty-four years old and the potential for her falling. Mary Lou went back into her room and we headed for the basement.

I felt Mary Lou had more experiences, but I knew we would have the opportunity to hear them once we returned from the basement. Anytime I enter a home or business that has claims of paranormal activity, my first question is, where do you experience the most activity? That is the area I want to go to first. So in this case, we headed to the basement.

Once we arrived in the basement, I explained to Todd and his daughter that I was going to ask a few questions to see if I could capture any responses on our digital recorder. I asked if I had permission to set up a camera to record in the basement.

Todd said, "Sure."

While I was setting up the equipment, Tina asked, "What if you don't get anything? I don't know what they do, but I assume they would be smart enough. Apparently, whenever I am down here by myself, I hear things and see things, and when I go get Dad, he comes down, and it's gone, nothing. Apparently, they don't want Dad to know. What if they don't come near at all because it knows? It doesn't show up because they know."

Tami asked Tina, "Do you mean when the Medium shows up?"

Todd said, "No, when I'm here." Todd now looked at Tina and said, "When they are ready, I can go upstairs. You can stay down with them and I can go up. They just want somebody here with them, so I'll go upstairs and maybe something will happen."

Tina agreed.

I asked Tina, "Can you explain to us what you feel and see in the basement when you are down here?"

Tina pointed beside the pool table where we were standing and said, "In the middle of the wall, I saw a black figure standing and it just looked at me."

I asked her, "Can you tell who it is or if it's male or female?"

Tina said, "No, it's only a black figure. At times when I am doing my artwork, I feel someone is watching me."

I pressed record on both video and audio. I set the digital audio recorder on the pool table. Todd told us he would be right back and went upstairs. Tina stood at one end of the pool table while Tami and I stood to one side, almost at the other end of the table. I started the session by saying, "We are here because this family is experiencing spirit activity and we want to give them answers to why this is happening. We mean no disrespect, and we are only here to help. Can you please give me your name? Why are you trying to get the attention of the people in this house? Tina sees you down here quite a few times. Why are you showing yourself to her? There is no reason to be afraid."

Tami asked Tina, "Have you ever noticed your dog bark at something that isn't there?"

Tina said, "Coco would stare at the top of the stairs like

something was there, then as he looks away, I can hear like light footsteps going up the stairs."

Tami pointed and asked, "Those steps right there?" She pointed to the basement steps we just came down.

Tina nodded and said, "Yes."

I now ask, "Can you please tell me your name? We are here to help. There has to be a reason you are touching Todd's mom. A reason why you are trying to get their attention. Did you live next door? This is your perfect opportunity. Any way we can help, we will gladly help. We will get your story out and convey any messages you want the family to know. Are you Todd's dad? Is there a message you want to give him?"

Tami looked at Tina and said, "What I want you to do is, if you feel, see, or hear anything, I just want you to say, you need to leave me alone. I cannot help you. This is my space and you need to leave." Tina nodded in agreement.

Todd came down the steps to join us again.

She asked Todd, "Is your mom on any medication that would cause her to experience some of the things that she perceives as paranormal such as the occurrences at night? She did say, though, that she felt a hand." Tami is a paramedic. When we are asked to go to homes which have paranormal activity, she always asks about medication.

Todd said, "No. Some things, I believe what she says, while other things, she may not just be remembering correctly." Todd began to tell us a story about when his mom had to go to the emergency room. He said, "You know when you go to the emergency room, you wait, wait, and wait. My mom was in one bed and this other woman was in a bed next to her. She was lying down, having a conversation with at least three, four, or five different people. Nobody was there, nobody that I could see. I really believe somebody was there. It looked like she was on her deathbed. I mean, she was talking like we are talking now, but nobody was there. When my mom said someone touched her arm, well, I believe that."

I added, "I believe everything your mom experienced."

Tami said, "The reason I am asking is due to the medical side of it. I sometimes think the patients I transport in the ambulance could be gifted, but their family members think they are out there."

Tami touched her index finger against her forehead and then points her arm forward to show the family thinks the person they are transporting is crazy. "They really aren't, and these people are actually connecting to the other side. Everyone around them is just writing it off."

Todd nodded his head in agreement as Tami talked.

I added, "I believe when someone is at that point, from being sick or whatever, I believe passed loved ones are coming to be with that person and guide or cross them over. I personally like to describe it as, 'walking them home.'"

There are many documented cases of people who are near death that have visions of passed loved ones or angels appearing in the room. Some in the scientific community might argue that these experiences are just the result of the medication the person is being administered at that time. This might be a reasonable conclusion, but what about the documented cases of the ones who weren't on any medications and experienced these same type of visions? Some believe it could be what happens as the brain is dying. Others, such as doctors, nurses, caregivers, or family, may have a different outlook.

They proclaim and believe that they are witnessing compelling proof of life after death. I find it really interesting that most people would be scared to see a ghost of their loved one during their daily life, but when it happens at the end of one's life, it seems to bring more of a calming and healing feeling to them. It is a very fascinating subject.

Todd agreed and said, "I think it's that way with my dad. He can't take her until it's her time. Normally, I would have, well, I've been talking to Jeff for a while now and I probably would have let it go, but she is seeing things more." He points to Tina. Then Todd points to the ceiling, meaning his mom upstairs. "She is hell-bent on moving back to the apartment above the garage. She isn't getting abused here or anything. I just don't want her alone anymore. Yes, she is right up there in the apartment, but it's not the same. I don't want to have to go up there and check on her three or four times a day. There is a reason why, I just don't know what it is. She just wants to go back up to that apartment, and I don't want that."

Todd felt since his dad was in the garage a lot, that maybe the reason his mom is so hell-bent on living there is because she would feel close to him being in that space.

Tami now changed the subject and asked Todd, "Who lives in that house across the street?" She points in the direction of that house.

Todd said, "My nephew's family."

I said, "We heard blaring old-time music coming from over there."

Tami added, "I'd say like the 1920s."

Todd had this puzzled look on his face as we mentioned the music.

Tami said, "Yeah, I called Jeff over to the other side of the truck and said listen to this. It reminded me of a time when people gathered around the radio since nobody had TVs."

Todd, still having the puzzled look on his face, said, "I didn't hear anything when I came out."

Todd pointed at me and said, "That's the house I told him that years ago it was said they had a sewing circle, women talking, like somewhere in that era. I only talked to the lady there a little. Something happened in the basement where they ripped out the walls and ceiling and put up new ones. She said they had the house cleansed." Todd shrugged his shoulders and said, "They had somebody come in, maybe like what we are doing here. I don't know. The day my dad died, I was mowing the grass over there and it kept feeling like someone in that attic was watching me or something was watching me. That day when I came home from work, the back door was open. My dad and I were always doing things in the garage, and it wasn't uncommon for him to lie down and take a nap. He had a stroke four years before that. After he had the stroke, he wasn't quite the same. Before that, he could do anything he wanted to do. He built this house. He could build anything without a blueprint. You tell him there was something wrong with something, he would take like an x-ray with his mind or whatever and he could fix it. He would know who was calling before the phone would ring. He would say, we haven't heard from so and so for a long time, then five minutes later, the phone would ring and it was them. But the day he died, I came home from work and the back door was unlocked. I didn't think nothing of it." Todd took a deep breath and said, "I went upstairs, changed into my old clothes, got my tractor and started mowing. It never dawned on me to check on him because he just told us he was going to be fine. We were out of the woods and there would be no worries. Well, three days later, I came home, didn't think anything about it, and went over there to mow. Every time I would be over there mowing, it always felt like someone was watching me. Every time except that day. That day my dad died. That part was odd. I liked having him around. I think my dad is watching us. I believe it's my dad here. He is watching over Tina, me, and my mom. I really believe it's him. I believe it could also be other people or spirits or whatever, but I truly believe he is here."

Todd now started to tell us about the neighbor lady that used to live in a trailer on the property right beside his house. Todd began to tell this story and stopped and pointed at his arm and said, "Look, it's giving me goosebumps. From what my dad said, the woman who lived there put a hex on my brother. That's when my dad put the broom at the front door to keep witches away. Whenever that was going on, she would be down there in that trailer and you could see her pacing back and forth. The way I understand it, that woman never came into this house. I just want to know what's going on in this house. Is there something scaring my mom, and she just isn't saying or what?"

It's always interesting to me to hear other people's beliefs, superstitions, and perspective. When Todd mentioned that his dad put a broom out front, that intrigued me. I figured since his family is Pennsylvania German, just as mine are, that it had to come from that line of belief.

One belief is, if bewitched, you are to lay a broom before the door. The first person to come along and pick it up is the witch.

There were other beliefs that by placing a broom over the door or beside it, keeps out bad intent and evil. It's a form of protection for the home and who lives there.

Todd told me that he just wants to figure out what is going on with his mom. He said, "I just figured you could pick up on something or maybe through your energy, she could pick up on something."

It seemed Todd was eager to find answers to why all this was happening now, since no similar paranormal activity happened in all the years living on this property.

Tina began to tell us a story of what she witnessed one night in her bedroom. She said it happened sometime last year. Tina said, "The one day, well, it was at night." As she is telling this story, she is pacing back and forth along the side of the pool table. As she is pacing, she grabs a white box to signify her nightstand and a jar of peanut butter which represented her cup. "I look up and it's three a.m., and of course they call that the witching hour." As she says this, Todd looks at me and shrugs his shoulder as if to say, *I don't know where she heard that, but she is right.* "I turned over to look at the time on my nightstand. I had a cup beside the clock. I watched my cup lift straight up, move and fall." As she explained this story, she had the peanut butter on top of the white box. She lifted it straight up about a foot in the air, moved it to the right about two feet, and dropped it. "It literally did that. It did that and that's not good."

The last sentence she said was kind of quieter as she put the box and jar back where she found them in the basement. I actually didn't pick up on her saying that until I watched the video recording later. I first thought, well, maybe the cup was wet, and it slid from the moisture underneath and she just witnessed that. Then I thought, well, she lifted it straight up and by her description, the cup moved through the air and dropped. Not only that, but it happened at precisely three a.m. Those two things made me take note in the event it happened again.

I believe what Tina said. Granted, Tina is only ten years old and kids have big imaginations, but Tina doesn't seem, to me, to be the same as most kids her age. I found Tina to be very articulate when she speaks. It was like talking to an adult in a kid's body. She seemed to be a very intelligent girl for her age.

Todd began to tell us about another experience his mom had. He said, "The bedroom I have now on the second floor used to be her bedroom. For years after..." Todd didn't finish the thought.

I felt he meant to say, years after his dad's passing.

Todd went on to say, "In that bedroom, she would feel her whole body getting lifted very close to the ceiling. She felt as if she was floating. She described it as being lifted off the bed and just floating. After my dad died, I knew she would have a lot of nightmares. I would hear this strange noise, something like in a horror film. She was making really weird sounds at least once a week. I would have to wake her up. This went on for quite a while, and I don't remember when it stopped."

I found the last two stories to be interesting because I was under the impression that the paranormal activity just recently started out of nowhere. By hearing the last two stories, it seemed to contradict that.

I asked Todd, "If you don't mind, I am going to ask some more questions to see if I can get some answers. Many times, I'll just have a normal discussion like we just were and Spirit will join in. We will capture any responses. It happens more times that way than asking specific questions, but I would like to try both just to see."

Todd agreed and said, "Yeah, you can do whatever you want."

I started this session by introducing ourselves. I said, "Todd asked us to come in here. His mom and daughter are seeing things, so can you tell me why you are here? Can you tell me your name? We don't mean any disrespect. We are just trying to understand why you are here? Is there something you need to say? Why are you trying to get their attention? If you do have a message, this is the perfect opportunity to do so, because that is why we are here. This is the perfect opportunity to tell us your story. Are you part of the property? Are you part of the family? Is there a reason Todd doesn't see you and his daughter does? Something you want to tell his daughter? Do you visit his mother? Can you make a noise to let us know you are here and that you hear me? We are just trying to figure it out and to help you. There is a reason why they are seeing you, so you must want to tell them something."

Todd told Tina he would be right back and went upstairs. I began to ask questions in reference to Tina. I asked, "Why do you show yourself to Tina? There is no reason to be afraid."

I also have a piece of equipment called the SB-7. I now took that out of my bag. This piece of equipment scans frequencies, and it is believed by many in the paranormal field to be a legitimate source to capture spirit communication. I usually set it to scan backward at the fastest rate. By doing this, it will scan multiple frequencies in seconds. One would think it would be impossible to capture a direct response to a question or receive a message, but we do when a spirit feels like communicating.

As Tami was explaining to Tina what this piece of equipment was used for, Todd came back down the steps. I explained that while the scanning was going on that they should listen to the voices under the scanning sound. I said, "There may be interference sometimes, but that should be ignored and only listen for things in the static." An external speaker had to be used since the speaker that comes with the SB-7 did not have sufficient volume controls. I started the SB-7. I asked the same questions as earlier but also asked, "Are you part of the family? Are you part of the property? Did you live here? Can you please tell me your name? Did you build this house? Don't be afraid. Please communicate with us. Just trying to understand."

Tami asked, "Who currently lives here?"

"Can you tell me somebody's name in this house?" I asked. "Can you tell me what year it is?"

During the session, we could hear what sounded like responses but couldn't make out what was said exactly. I told them that I would listen later and go over everything. We tried two different methods to capture audio evidence.

Todd said that nothing in the house scares them, but they want to find out what it was.

I asked Todd if we could spend some time with his mom to see if we could get some answers.

Todd said, "Yeah sure."

Tami and I packed up the equipment and headed back upstairs.

We went back up the stairs into the dining room, turned right to enter the kitchen and then made another right, which took us straight into the living room. We stopped at the front door and in front of Mary Lou's room. She was sitting in her chair with her back to us, continuing her crocheting as she was when we first arrived. Todd brought out pictures of his dad to show us. Todd said he had two brothers, a sister, and another sister who died at birth. Todd then pointed out pictures that were hanging on the wall in the living room. They were of his mom, her sister, and three brothers. When he pointed to the one picture and said the man's name on the far right, his mom's brother, Bobby, my left ear began to ring very loudly, which I took note of. I took note because I had come to realize that even though I had severe tinnitus, when my ear suddenly rings louder than usual, that was my sign of validation or that I should take notice of what was said.

Todd then walked across the living room and stopped at his mom's bedroom door. Todd asked her what Bobby's middle name was. Todd said the name Paul keeps coming up, and he asked her if his middle name was Paul.

Mary Lou said, "No, that was Richard Simon, and Bobby was Robert Leroy."

Todd asked his mom, "Pappy, whose name was Simon, what was his middle name?" Mary Lou's mind seemed to go blank, and she couldn't recall.

Todd said, "Simon would be your dad's name."

Mary Lou said, "Yeah." She sighed and said, "I'm so used to calling him Pappy."

We laughed and Tami said, "We are making you work hard today, huh?"

Mary Lou said, smiling, "Yeah." She placed her hands in her pockets and sighed.

Todd told her, "It's okay if you can't think of it. His name isn't Paul, right? His middle name isn't Paul?"

Mary Lou said, "No, but I had an uncle Paul."

Todd asked, "What did he look like? Did he have three kids, wore a hat, glasses? He walked kinda hunched over a bit?"

Mary Lou said, "Yes."

Todd asked, "Would he possibly have used a lantern?"

Mary Lou said, "Yeah, probably, because they didn't have things like this." She pointed at the lights. Mary Lou said, "His name was Paul Klouser."

Todd began to tell his mom about when Tami and I were sitting out in our truck and we heard music from possibly the 1920s or '30s.

Tami walked to the bay window in Mary Lou's room and pointed down the street. As she pointed, she said, "It sounded like it was coming from that house right there."

"'There was always something unusual about that place," Todd said as he was looking at his mom.

Mary Lou agreed and said, "There was a man that died over there. He was very very sick when we moved here. I remember that because they had a phone and we didn't, so if we needed to call anyone, Donald would go across the street and call from there."

Todd said, "I did not know that."

Mary Lou then began to tell us of things that happened to her that she couldn't explain. She told us again that while she was sleeping, someone lifted her arm and dropped it. She said she didn't know who it was or why they were doing it. She went on to tell us that on one occasion she got up from her bed to walk over to the space heater in her room, which was about three feet from the bottom of her bed. She said, "As I was walking over, I felt someone grab my waist, turn me, and guide me back to my bed and lay me down."

I asked her, "How did it feel? Was it done nicely or forcibly?"

She said, "No, it was done very easy and caring, like it was looking out for me."

This really interested me. I wondered who it was that helped Mary Lou back to her bed. I felt it had to be someone from her family. It was very important to Mary Lou as well, since she told us this story twice.

Todd said he wanted to take us to the garage before we had to leave. He told his mom we would be back, and that we were just going to the garage.

As we walked out of her room, we stopped in the living room just in front of Mary Lou's bedroom doorway. Mary Lou brought out pictures and was showing them to Tami. Holding one picture, Mary Lou told Tami, "These are the beams when we were building the house after the house burned."

She was interrupted by Tami asking, "So, this house burned?"

Todd explained, "It didn't burn down to the ground. It was just cosmetic."

Mary Lou pointed and said, "This door was closed, and that door was closed." She first pointed to her bedroom door, then to the back door.

Tami pointed out that it's said to keep your doors closed in case of a fire.

Mary Lou nodded her head yes and said, "I always wanted the doors open, but I was glad they were closed that day."

Todd said, "Since the fire, I have smoke alarms throughout the house. I had one in the kitchen, but it always went off when there was cooking, so I moved it."

Tami looked at Mary Lou and said, "That's how I know dinner is done... when the smoke alarm goes off."

Mary Lou laughed and said, "Yeah."

Todd began telling us of when he woke up to a fire in the house back in the nineties. He said, "I always felt that it was my dad that woke me up. The fire caused internal damage, but nothing structural." Todd recalled how the fire happened. He said, "I worked the third shift at the time. She wasn't home." He pointed to his mom. "I was sleeping. I had my room as dark as it could be."

Tami agreed, knowing what it was like working the third shift and trying to sleep in the daytime.

Todd said, "I was lying on my back and it was like someone grabbed my shirt. I woke up as I was sitting up. It sounded like the hot-air furnace that's in the garage was twice as loud and it wasn't burning right. I didn't smell smoke at all. I opened the bedroom door and the upstairs hallway was so thick with smoke. If I held my hand out in front of me, I wouldn't have seen it. I slammed the door shut and tried to get my breath because my lungs filled up immediately."

Todd made this sound like he was just being resuscitated and gasping for breath.

Todd said, "I climbed out my bedroom window and got some air. That was the year we had so much snow and roofs were collapsing. Prior to the fire, people thought I was crazy, but I was trying to get that weight off the roofs."

Tami said, "There is a reason you felt you needed to do that."

Todd agreed and said, "Yes, I'm glad I did that now. All I had to do was jump down five feet, then another five feet to the ground. I ran down to my sister's next door. All I had on were socks and one of these on," he said as he pointed to the flannel shirt he was wearing. "I pounded on her door. I told her to call 9-1-1, that the house was on fire."

Of course, she was in a panic immediately and was saying, "Where's my phone? Where's my phone?"

I said, "Patty, your phone is in your hand."

She called 9-1-1, and all she said was, "Send somebody quick. My mother's house is on fire!"

"There wasn't much discussion, but somehow they figured out where she lived and who it was and everything. They don't know for sure the cause of the fire, but they believe it was bad wiring in the bathroom. There wasn't a whole lot of fire, it was mostly smoke. We gutted the whole house. Took out all the drywall, all the insulation due to the smoke and water damage."

I took note of this and wanted to see if Claire would say anything related to a fire.

Tami and I stood there for a minute or two. I turned and didn't see Mary Lou or Tina, either. Tami and I took a few steps and walked into the doorway between the kitchen and dining room. We didn't see anyone. As I looked across the kitchen, I saw Mary Lou slowly walk from right to left and into the bathroom. As I watched her walk, I was taken aback because to me, it honestly looked like I was watching a spirit walk across the opposite side of the kitchen. Just the way she moved slowly and expressionless looked as if I was watching ghost footage on a television show or on the internet. I really thought this was strange.

Todd then walked into the kitchen, saying he didn't know where they were. He said, "I want to show you the garage quick before you leave."

As we turned to walk out the kitchen door to the garage, I looked across the room to see if I could see Mary Lou walk back out, but I didn't see her. I kept thinking, did I really see her? That image would forever be in my mind.

We walked out to the garage and looked around while Todd explained how he and his dad had built it. He talked about all the projects they did together in it. He thought maybe we would capture evidence in the garage of his dad, since his dad spent a lot of time in it. After reviewing the video, nothing was captured on video or audio. As we headed back to the house, we stopped in front of the garage. Todd began to tell me more about the witch story he started telling us in the basement. Todd said as he pointed, "Before that house was built, there was a trailer there. I mentioned my dad would tell us that the woman who lived there was a witch. My dad didn't like them and swore up and down that she was a witch. My brother told me when she died, her husband had her cremated and put her ashes in like a baked bean can or something and buried her in the front yard by the tree. After that house was sold, there was another couple there, and the woman had really bad asthma. You have to remember back in the sixties and seventies, they didn't have the things they do now for that. She actually committed suicide on that property. She ran a hose into her car and died by carbon monoxide poisoning. She killed herself on that property in her car, in the driveway, because she just couldn't take it any longer. They said she was in so much pain. Later, the place was sold to another couple. Five to seven years later, my sister bought it. It was either my sister or the prior couple who asked my dad to dig up the can and put it in the woods all the way in the back corner. They just threw it in."

In disbelief, I yelled, "What? Oh my God! They just threw the can with her ashes randomly in the woods?"

Todd said, "They just went up there and threw it in the woods. The trailer was later removed and that house was built."

Todd pointed to the house again.

Todd said, "Before the house was built, her ashes were dug up and reburied behind our garage in the back woods."

I wondered if she really was a witch and if so, did moving her ashes have anything to do with any of the visions I've had?

We headed back into the house, went into the living room, and began to put our equipment away. Mary Lou came out of her room, holding a picture frame. She had an expression of happiness and love as she carried the frame. Her face lit up as she showed Tami her wedding picture. The love she had for her husband was evident. She then explained how she was the last one of all her family left. She said, "I don't know why I can't go to be with them, and I don't understand why I am the only one left?"

Tami told her, "There are a few that need you yet." As Tami said this, she pointed to Todd and Tina.

I felt bad for Mary Lou because I could not only see what she said truly bothered her, but I felt it. It had to be hard to be the last living person of all her brothers, sisters, and husband, and wonder why you were the only one left? This answer, Mary Lou really wanted to know.

We thanked them all again for letting us into their home. I told them I would go over all audio and video footage to see if we captured any evidence, then I would let them know. We walked to our truck. After talking a bit more beside the truck, we backed up and pulled away. Seeing Mary Lou come out of her bedroom after we returned from the garage was a good sign to me after the image of her walking slowly across the kitchen. What I saw I didn't mention at the time, to Tami on the way home, or at all, until I wrote this book. It was just something I kept to myself and I'm not really sure why.

Chapter 3

Knock Knock

I immediately began to go over all the audio and video when I arrived home. When Tami and I were asking questions in the basement, there were three distinct knocks coming from the direction of the bar, which was on the opposite side of the room from the pool table where we were all standing. When I asked, "Did you live next door?" There was a knock. I said, "This is the perfect opportunity." There was a knock. I asked, "Are you Todd's father? Is there a message that you want to give him?" There was another knock. I remember hearing the knocks, but thought maybe it was a normal house sound, but after listening, now I wasn't sure. While watching the video footage when these knocks occurred, Tina and Tami both reacted to them and looked over in the direction of the sound. During our SB-7 session, there were two responses to our questions. There was a male response that we heard at the time but couldn't tell what was being said. After listening, it was still difficult to understand. It is definitely a male response to the question. The other response was when I asked, "Can you tell me someone's name in this house?" A female replies with what sounds to be a very clear, "Baby doll." I played the file for Todd the very next day and he agreed it sounds like baby doll.

I asked him, "Did your dad ever call your mom baby doll? Have you ever called your daughter that or was that name familiar to anyone in the home?"

Todd said, "No, it was never used to my knowledge."

I told him, "Even though it seems like nothing makes sense yet, many pieces of the puzzle will come together more once the Medium conducts her walkthrough."

During the week leading up to the walkthrough with the Medium, I wanted to do some research to see what I could find out about the property. First, I did a deed search and found out who the owners of the house and the property were. My search took me back to the 1930s. It seems there were land transactions, but not until 1968 was there a deed for a home. I looked at the date again and it stated, March 26, 1968. I thought, wait a minute, and double-checked the day we were asked to go to Todd's house for the first time. I found it fascinating that the day we were asked to come over was the fiftieth anniversary of when his parents bought the property or possibly built the home. When I told Todd, he thought the same as I. This was no coincidence. We both felt it was meant to be. This would end up being one of many things that happened that were not a coincidence but was meant to be.

My next step was to try and contact the local historical society to see what they may know of the property and the surrounding area.

I spoke to a man named Jim Freeman. I found it interesting that his last name of Freeman was also Todd's father's middle name. Jim was very friendly and informative. We ended up talking for about an hour on the phone.

Every little bit of information helps to put the puzzle together. He told me that many years ago there was a tannery in that area. He believed two people died in an explosion. He said back in those days, there were many small homes called bungalows in that area and in the area that is now the lake. He went on to say that Calcium Road, on the other side of the lake, and the road to the house in question were once the same road, but when they built the Ontelaunee Lake, most of that road disappeared and is covered by the lake. I found this to be very fascinating as well. The Calcium Road he spoke of, I lived on that road and it has been involved with my family for over thirty years.

This house is where my interest in the paranormal began. This home is very haunted, and now I know that the road we lived on and the road Todd lives on were at one time the same road until separated by the man-made lake back in 1926.

Prior to that, you could travel straight across. Jim told me that the road is still there, and when they made the lake, many things like part of the homes, roads, and even poles were left. They just filled it in with water to form the lake. After he said this, I remember back in the early 90s, there was a drought and the lake got so low that we could almost walk across it. We saw foundations of homes, steps, roads, etc. that were underneath the lake all this time, just as Jim said. We have pictures of how low the lake was and the remnants left behind. One spot, I remember sitting on steps that went to a house that wasn't there. Only the steps and the foundation remained. I even remember walking down a road which should have been under water.

This rock foundation became visible during a drought. Lake Ontelaunee.

This road became visible during a drought. Lake Ontelaunee.

Jim told me of a mill that was on the edge at Todd's side of the lake. I also learned that the one meeting house that is just below Todd's house was originally just below our old house. They moved it over to Todd's side when the lake was built. This Quaker meeting house dates back to the 1700s. Jim gave me a website to look for old maps of the area. After our lengthy conversation, I thanked him for his time and the information.

Chapter 4

Medium Arrives

March 31, 2018, we arrived about an hour earlier than Claire so we could go over a few items that I found during my research and play the files of audio that we captured the previous Monday.

We do this regularly because we want to keep the homeowner informed and at the same time we don't want any Medium that conducts a walkthrough to have any prior knowledge of the property whatsoever. The only thing a Medium will know prior is we send a picture of the home to whomever is going to do the walkthrough and we send the address just a few hours prior to their scheduled arrival. This is very important to us. We want the walkthrough to be authentic, and we don't want any information to influence the Medium prior to her walkthrough.

I walked out onto the porch as Claire pulled into the driveway. On the porch was an old school desk which sat at the edge of the steps leading to the porch. As she walked past it, she stopped. She pointed to it and asked, "Where did this come from?"

I said, "I have no idea, why?"

She said, "I feel negative energy attached to it and it needs to be cleansed. I wonder if it was in a building that had a fire at one time because I feel fire connected to it."

I asked Todd, "Where did that desk come from?"

Todd said, "I got it at the Leesport Farmers' Market. I don't want it anymore anyway, so I will get rid of it."

Claire told Todd she would cleanse it before leaving. This was important to me because she picked up on a fire. Was she feeling the fire connected to the desk or to the house in general, considering the fire started on that side of the house? I told Claire, "Nothing is off-limits and you can go in any area you get pulled or drawn to. Let's get this party started," I said as we opened the front door.

We entered the home and walked into the living room. I asked a friend, Steve, and his daughter, Natalya, to join us because Natalya is coming into her gift. I thought her experiencing a haunted home during the walkthrough would help her understand and I get to see how she reacts to the energy in the home. Steve and Natalya were waiting in the living room. I asked Steve if he wouldn't mind holding the digital audio recorder as we walked around so I had another source of audio. During an investigation or walkthrough, it is always good to have more than one audio and video source. That way potential evidence captured could be validated or dismissed. I looked at Claire and she was swaying side to side then leaned far back. I asked, "Is the energy knocking you over?"

Claire said, "It's a lot."

She shifted her eyes and head side to side quickly.

Claire always burns sage as she conducts her walkthrough. Each Medium that joins us has different ways of conducting their walkthrough. They may burn sage, write in a tablet, or just close their eyes as they connect to Spirit. We were concerned about the sage smoke affecting Mary Lou due to her being in her eighties. After Claire lit the sage and the smoke began to filter around, Mary Lou said that it did not bother her so we were good to go. Claire then walked over to the doorway of Mary Lou's room and waved the sage smoke to the corner at the left side of the doorway. While she did this, she said a few sentences that were just whispers and could not be understood. Since this wasn't my first time with her in a home, I knew the words she was saying were to rid the house of any spirits that were not of high vibration. Good spirits vibrate at a higher frequency and so-called bad spirits will vibrate at a lower frequency. Everything is energy, vibration, and frequency. To understand the universe and the spirit world, one must think of these three things. We always ask the homeowner to not tell the Medium anything unless she asks and to let her go in any direction she is led to, without influencing her.

Claire started the walkthrough by getting pulled into Mary Lou's room. As she walked in, the first thing she said was, "I'm getting that male again."

I asked, "Same guy you mentioned before? The guy in his thirties, early forties?"

She said, "Yeah, but closer to thirty." Claire asked me, "Do you know who lived here prior?"

I explained, "This family built this house and there wasn't a house here prior to building it. That isn't saying there wasn't a building one hundred years ago or anything, just not that I know of."

Claire said, "No, he isn't going back that far."

I asked Claire, "Is he connected to the property or the family?"

She said, "It feels more like the property."

Behind her, Todd stood in the doorway. He was shaking his head no as she described this guy. He said, "We don't know anyone like that." Todd was still very adamant about not knowing anyone named Paul.

Claire asked, "Was there an accident out front here?"

Todd stood in the doorway, shaking his head.

I asked her, "Was it a car or motorcycle?"

Claire replied, "Truck." Claire turned toward the bay window facing Shoemakersville road and said, "I feel like it was out here." She waved her feather left to right in the direction of the road. "I feel he came here. He has been here a long time. I get the late sixties. When was the house built?"

Todd said, "1968."

Claire looked at me as if to say, I knew it and there is the validation. Claire turned to Mary Lou. "Do you remember an accident at all?"

Mary Lou didn't hear her fully, so I asked her, "Do you remember a car accident or any kind of accident with a truck?"

Mary Lou, who was on the opposite side of the room at the time, said, "Yes."

I was shocked and turned to look at Mary Lou. I asked, "Seriously?"

She said, "Yes, it was out front here. They went over the embankment and hit the tree. My husband went out in his underwear and helped them out of the vehicle."

Claire asked her, "Did anyone die in it?"

Mary Lou said, "No."

"Are you sure?" Claire asked.

Mary Lou said, "I don't know what happened to him later."

Claire replied under her breath, "He died because he is here."

Mary Lou said, "Excuse me, but I have a question." She looked at me. "Last time you were here, you mentioned a guy by the name of Paul."

I said, "Yes, why?"

She said, "Well, the guy that was in the accident was named Paul."

We were all like, holy shit, you got to be kidding me, and started high-fiving each other. Wow, now that was validation! I had full body chills at that moment.

Steve had a look of amazement and said, "Wow, now that's validation."

I said to Todd, "Now the pieces of the puzzle will slowly fall into place."

Claire asked Mary Lou, "Did you know him?"

She said, "Yes, he was a friend of the neighbor that used to live across the street and would come over here. Many times he would sit on the porch with the men and they would have a good time."

Claire asked her, "Did Paul look at you like a mother figure?"

Mary Lou said, "Yes."

Claire said, "He is here, and he is just looking out for you and likes the energy in the house." She asked Mary Lou, "Do you experience things in your bedroom?"

Mary Lou said, "Yes, I feel someone rock the bed and someone lifts my arm up then drops it." Mary Lou pointed to where Claire was standing which was on the right side of the bed if you are standing at the foot of the bed. Mary Lou said, "Where you are standing, a man stands once in a while."

Claire asked Mary Lou, "Do you know what he looks like?"

Mary Lou said, "Yes, he is well dressed. He is not in dungarees or a t-shirt like my husband wore. He was in a suit and he stands right there." She pointed to where Claire is standing.

Claire told Mary Lou, "The person you see is related to you. This man talks to you. Do you hear him?"

Mary Lou said, "No, he doesn't say anything. He stands there so I just turnover."

Claire said, "He is saying, Mary, be careful. Mary, watch it, be careful." Claire asked Mary, "Do you ever get dizzy?"

Mary Lou said, "Yes, sometimes." Mary Lou began to tell us how she walked to the heater the one day. Someone grabbed her hips, turned her, guided her back to bed and helped her lie down.

Claire said, "That was your brother, Richard. He is looking out for you and trying to keep you safe. It's all love. He is trying to protect you and keep you from falling."

Mary Lou agreed and said, "He and I were this close." She extended her right arm out and crossed her middle and index finger to symbolize they were close. "My dad would say, where you find one, you'd find the other."

Claire asked, "Is there another Mary?"

Todd said, "No."

Mary Lou said, "Yes, she was my stepmother."

Claire asked Mary Lou, "Was she more of a mother figure?"

Mary Lou said, "Yes, more so."

Claire asked if Mary Lou fell at all. Claire said she felt the spirits are trying to protect her from falling.

I told Todd to take that as a fair warning. Todd asked what I meant.

I said, "There is a reason the spirits are communicating that and you need to take it seriously. We have free will, but take what she said seriously and watch out for your mom because something may happen soon."

Claire asked Mary Lou, "Do you have two brothers on the other side?"

Mary Lou nodded her head and said, "Two brothers and my husband."

As she said this, Claire cut in and said, "Yeah, you have a lot. There are many spirits that come and go in this room and they are all family. What you are feeling in here is passed loved ones and that Paul."

Mary Lou said, "I'm not afraid. I'm definitely not afraid. That's what I told Christina when she saw something, don't be afraid. They aren't going to hurt you."

Claire nodded her head in agreement and said, "So far, it's passed loved ones and they mean no harm at all. They actually love you and want to protect you. They want to keep you on your feet."

Mary Lou nodded as she laughed and said, "Ok, I'm eighty-four so they got a job ahead of them."

The room broke out in laughter as she said that.

Claire told Mary Lou, "They make me feel you are in danger, that you may fall and break a hip."

I asked Claire, "Where are you getting drawn to next?"

She said, "Left. Is there a hallway?" Claire walked out of Mary Lou's bedroom and turned left.

As we walked toward the direction of the basement, she stopped and looked to the right and up the stairs. She mentioned she was getting drawn there as well.

Todd told her she can go wherever she feels she should go.

Claire now turned to Natalya and asked, "When I was getting that stuff in there, what were you feeling?"

Natalya replied, "I didn't feel much. I felt really hot. I don't know if anyone else felt it, but my hands were really sweaty. I'm not nervous or anything, but it just feels weird."

Claire said, "Yeah, you just described me. You are feeling the physical symptoms that I'm feeling. Have you heard anything?"

Natalya shook her head and said, "Not so far."

Claire continued to walk and wave the sage smoke around the room as everyone's eyes stayed focused on her. She turned from across the kitchen and said in a whisper, "I need to go there." She pointed the feather at the doorway to the dining room.

As soon as you enter the dining room and turn left, that is where the steps to the basement are located. Claire turned left immediately and walked down the stairs.

Claire stopped at the bottom of the steps and said, "I feel a female presence." She then made a right into the one basement room. She took a few steps and turned, facing the room. She said, "It's a strong female presence."

Todd and Tina were sitting on the middle steps while we stood in the room. This side of the steps was open to the room, but the other side was covered by a wall. She looked at Todd and Tina and asked, "Do you see something on the steps?"

Todd said, "The dog does. When I am down here watching TV and Tina is doing her crafts, the dog will stare at the steps."

Tina then added, "Yeah and when that happens you can hear someone walking up and down the steps."

Claire was staring across the room and seemed to be in deep thought.

Natalya mentioned, "I am having a really weird feeling in my stomach."

Claire said, "Feels like we are playing hide and go seek a little bit."

Claire began to walk to the opposite side of the room. As she was walking, she said, "I feel the presence of a child, a girl." Claire asked, "Do things make noises down here like toys?"

Tina answered and said, "Not necessarily toys, but sounds we don't hear normally."

Claire asked, "Like crackling or pops?"

Tina replied, "Yeah, kinda."

Todd began to explain about experiences in the apartment above the garage.

Todd told Claire, "Prior tenants of that apartment would have toys that randomly would turn on and there was no explanation."

Claire nodded and then looked at me and asked, "So, you don't know what was here?"

I said, "I am in the middle of researching and I don't know for sure but I have ideas."

She then asked, "What do you think?"

I said, "I don't know for sure. What do you think?"

I am always hesitant to say anything I know or have seen myself to any Medium because I want them to say it first. I do not want to influence them in any way. It is more validating for them, myself, and to the homeowner if they are told the minimum until after the walkthrough or after they hit the nail on the head with what Spirit tells them.

Claire looked at me and asked, "Is it 1800s?"

I said, "Yeah."

She said, "It feels like children."

I asked, "How many?"

She said, "I got a glimpse of kids, boy, girl, and like a toddler, but they are all in long nightshirts."

I asked, "Three kids?"

She said, "I think it's only three kids." She looked at me smiling and said, "What?" She knew she hit something with me.

I said, "I don't want to say anything just yet. I can't. I just can't."

She arched her head back, rolled her eyes, turned, and walked away smiling.

I said, "It just blows me away honestly." I took a deep breath. I was speechless and in awe of what I just heard. I didn't want to tell her yet that I had a vision of three kids. It looked to me like two girls and a younger boy. It appeared to be around dusk and took place in the yard. The father was a few feet away from me on my right. He had a lantern in his hand. The three children were standing on his right side, the oldest one down to the youngest. They were wearing oversized shirts like nightshirts. They were opposite of me on an angle, facing where the street would be today.

Claire turned away from me as she began to walk to the back of the room. As she walked back, she said, "It feels sadder as I go back. It feels like it's coming up like from the ground."

I said, "Well, I can tell you now about that." I explained how this house was built on limestone and shale. There was a lot of it.

Todd added, "This foundation is built on solid rock."

This fact can be a very important piece to why this or any property is experiencing spirit activity. Limestone is said to be a catalyst for it. I asked, "What business or businesses do you feel may have been on this property?"

Claire said, "Hotel, tavern, people coming and going, boarding house, something like that."

At this point, she was standing in the doorway between one side room in the basement and the other. She turned, had the look of disgust on her face, and said, "I just seen a man hanging from a tree."

Claire asked, "Are there older trees behind the house and on the property?"

Todd said, "No."

She said, "It feels back and up, back, back."

Todd said, "The only tree is the one across the street and that goes way back."

I asked her again, "What was here?"

Claire said, "Meeting house maybe. People coming and going."

I told her, "There is a meeting house about half a mile from here, but nothing on this property."

She said, "It feels like a lot of yelling like a trial. They accused and they hanged somebody."

I asked, "Out back here?"

She said, "Yeah, I wouldn't know why else they are showing it to me."

Claire asked Natalya how she was feeling.

Natalya said, pointing to the front of the room, "Back there, I got the chills from nowhere at all."

Claire walked through the doorway and into the other side room.

There is a bar directly in front of this doorway.

She walked around the bar, waving the sage smoke. She said, "I feel the whole thing was hush, hush." She was referring to the accused and the hanging. She asked if anyone felt the cold change in the room?

I said, "No."

Todd stated, "This room is usually the warmer room."

Steve said, "It feels colder and I have a sweater on."

Claire now walked around the bar area, waving the sage smoke while saying, "If you are not of the light, you must leave now. I command you in the name of Jesus Christ to leave this house and this property. If you are attached or bound in any way, I ask Saint Michael and the Heavenly Father to remove those binds. I rebuke you to where you belong." She continued to walk around the room with sage and said, "In the name of Jesus Christ, I command you to leave this house. You are not welcome here."

Todd said, "It actually does feel a little colder in here."

Claire walked behind Tina and said, "Honey, just stay still for a moment." Claire stood behind Tina and waved the sage smoke around her.

Steve said, "It almost feels as if we walked into an air conditioner."

I asked Claire, "Do you think we will capture any audio?"

She said, "Yeah, but I thought you would before, but you didn't."

I said, "Well, actually, we did on Monday, but I didn't tell you what it was."

Claire arched her head back again as we both laughed.

Todd asked Claire, "Do you want to know where Tina saw the figure?"

Claire said, "Yes."

Tina said, "He was standing by the bird cage."

The bird cage was on the other side of this room across from the bar. It was on the side of the pool table along the front wall and about three feet tall.

Tina said, "The figure was by the bird cage, and I was standing by the door."

Claire asked, "Can you describe him for me?"

Tina said, "Thin, like Slender Man, but not as tall."

Claire asked, "Who is Slender Man?"

We all tried explaining who this is. Steve went on his phone to get a picture so Claire could understand what Tina was describing.

Tina went on to say, "White face, black body."

Claire asked her, "How did you feel when you saw it?"

Tina replied, "Startled at first when I saw it."

I asked, looking at Tina, "You said white face, black body?"

Tina nodded her head and said, "Mmm hmm."

Steve took a few steps and reached out his arm to Claire to show her a picture of the Slender Man that he found on his phone.

She nodded and then looked at Tina and asked her, "Could you see clothing?"

Tina said, "Just a pitch-black body."

Claire asked, "Was the white, was it a face or could it have been cloth? Did it have a shape of a head?"

Tina said, "Yeah, you could see the shape of the head, indents in eyes and stuff, but it was just like completely white."

The whole time as this conversation was going back and forth, I was in total amazement and wasn't sure whether to interrupt or keep listening. Reason being was just this morning I had a vision of what they were describing. I was in complete awe as they were describing the actual thing I had seen, and they had no idea yet that I saw it.

Claire asked, "Was there a tie at the neck?"

Tina said, "No."

This whole time I'm replaying the vision in my head but listening to them at the same time.

Claire asked, "Did the white just blend with the black?"

Tina said, "No, it was just like painting a picture, a white face and head, then stops at the neck, and then black."

By this time, I couldn't take it anymore and had to speak up. I interrupted and said, "I saw this person this morning! That's insane!"

Claire asked, "Could you see features though?"

I said, "No, I just saw a totally black body. Head was round and white. It really stood out. It was white. A chalky white is what I had seen."

Claire looked at me and said, "That's what I saw hanging from a tree. The white was the cloth they had over his head!"

I said, "That's crazy! I had just seen that this morning! I just got the chills again!"

Steve said, "Yeah, I just got the chills on my neck." He rubbed his neck and smiled.

To explain my vision this morning... I first saw people moving about a field. I couldn't see details because they were silhouettes. They seemed to be bending over, picking up things. I couldn't see what they were picking up or why they kept bending over. The vision then faded to a man beside a tree. He looked to be set there, slumped over, leaning to his left. His shoulder and his head were leaning on the tree. His body was all black. His face was chalky white. I didn't see any features which struck me to be odd. The contrast of black and his white head really stood out. I was standing what seemed like about forty yards from this person and the tree in the vision. His white head was leaning against the tree and facing in my direction.

As I am looking at him, the background flashed as lightning struck and lit up the sky. This lightning flashed twice. This vision stuck with me all day, and now I am standing in this house, listening to Claire and Tina describe what I had seen. I was amazed by the validation.

Sketch of the hanged man I saw in a vision.

The lightning still didn't make sense to me. Neither Claire, Tina, nor anyone else brought up lightning. I didn't either at this point, but within a week, it would all make sense. I told Claire, "You said you saw three kids. I had a vision of three kids. I wonder if it was the same three kids."

She asked, "Were they in nightshirts?"

I said, "Yes. It was a night setting. It was nighttime. I can tell you that." I said with relief, "I am so glad you validated that!"

She said laughing, "See you're not totally crazy, Jeff! They were in bed, going to bed, or getting out of bed. It was a nighttime-bed-time scenario."

I said, "That's why I couldn't wait for today because obviously I want to help them." I pointed to Todd. "There are things I want to do to help her," I said, pointing to Natalya. "Plus, I want to validate things that I saw."

Claire asked Tina, "Do you see other things in the house?"

Tina nodded and said, "Mmm hmm."

Claire asked, "In your bedroom?"

Tina said, "Yes."

"It is where we need to go next," Claire said. She asked Tina, "Do you get woken up at night?"

Tina said, "Yes."

We began to walk across the room to the stairs. I asked Claire, "Could you possibly, before we leave or sometime after, tell me more about the kids you saw and anything that was on this property?"

Claire nodded her head in agreement.

We walked up two flights of stairs and entered Tina's bedroom.

The room is a typical ten-year-old girl's bedroom.

Claire walked to the opposite right corner to the closet door, turned around, and asked Tina, "What's with the closet door? Does it open?"

Tina said, "No."

"The door doesn't open sometimes?" Claire asked.

Tina said, "No, it's always closed."

Claire said, "Standing here, I get the sensation that the door opens." Then she just shrugged her shoulders.

I asked Todd, "Do you have any problem with any door here that opens?"

Todd said, "No."

Tina chimed in and said, "The only time a door stayed open was when I was downstairs and saw that figure. I ran upstairs and waited because I knew something was going to happen and then the door opened."

Claire nodded and went onto another question. She asked, "What was it you had seen in here? Was it female?"

Tina replied, "I can't quite tell what it was. I'm going to be honest, I could barely even see it, but the one day I woke up, on the nightstand I had a cup, I saw it lift, move to the side, and drop."

Claire asked if it was kind of glowing. Tina said, "No."

Claire tried to describe it more and said, "It wasn't black, maybe kind of gray. It looked like a cloud."

Tina agreed and said, "Kinda, yeah, but it wasn't really clear though."

Claire, still trying to describe it better to Tina, said, "Like you could see through it like a real thin cloud. I don't know how else to describe it."

Tina agreed and said, "Yeah."

Claire began to walk to her right toward the other side of the room. She stopped and looked at Tina and asked, "Do you hear singing?"

Tina shook her head and said, "No."

I asked Claire, "Do you hear singing?"

She said, "Yeah. I can't really tell, but I think it has to do with those kids. It's like a lullaby, like um... old. I almost want to say hymn-like."

I asked her, "Can you tell... Obviously this house was built in the '60s, but can you see the house or anything on the property that was here? Did the spirits tell you anything?"

Claire replied, "Well, the house is like two stories with a porch, kinda like a flat roof, but there is a porch with a roof over it. Nothing fancy or anything, just kinda plain. I feel like people came, stayed overnight, passing through like a boarding house."

Steve walked over and relit the sage.

It is something that has to be done for Claire at every walk-through, and this day, it was Steve who had the honors, so to speak. After it was relit, Claire walked around the room, mumbling to herself and waving the sage smoke around with her feather. She walked around the one side of the bed to the foot of the bed, and then came walking toward me at the doorway. She stopped a few feet from me and said, "I feel a woman's presence."

I asked her, "Is it family or from the land?"

She said, "It feels connected to him," as she points to Todd. She began to describe what she felt. She said, "Grandmother on your dad's side."

Todd said, "I don't remember. She died sometime before I was born. I do not remember her. I don't have many memories either of my dad's father because he died when I was in the fifth grade."

She said, "I feel like it's someone who died. She wasn't old, like maybe sixty. Could be an aunt, but I'm not sure. It's protective." She pointed to Tina who was sitting on her bed. "She kinda hangs out there too sometimes." She pointed to the hallway.

Todd asked if she felt it was his father that woke him when the fire started.

Claire paused and then looked at me and said, "So there was a fire here? Wonder if that's why I got the fire out there on the porch?"

While she said this, her facial expression told me that she knew I was withholding information.

I said, "I'm sorry. I just can't tell you stuff."

Shaking her head and smiling, she asked, "Why can't you tell me stuff?"

I said, "Because it is more validation for them. I can't influence anything. I won't tell anybody anything."

She looked at Todd and said, "Yes, that was him." She was referring to his dad. She said to Todd, "You think and talk to him in your mind a lot?"

Todd said, "Yeah."

Claire said, "He hears you. You had dreams of him since he's been gone, correct?"

Todd said, "Yeah." Todd went on to say that this was his room before Tina came along. He looked at Claire and asked, "Was it him that shook the bed?"

She walked to the foot of the bed and went to sit down. As she sat, she asked, "Was it like sitting?"

Todd said, "Yes, and it was that corner." He referred to exactly where she was sitting.

Claire asked, "Was it at a time that you really needed him?"

Todd said, "I don't remember."

She said, "Yes, he wanted to let you know his presence is here."

Todd said, "I know it was his voice, and it was a long time ago." Todd said jokingly, "Tell him if he could help do the maintenance around here, I'd greatly appreciate it!"

Everyone laughed.

Claire said, "He is the reason why we are here."

Todd replied, "I figured."

We now walked into Tina's art/playroom, which is next to her bedroom. Claire walked around the entire room, burning the sage, and waving the smoke into all directions including the top corners of each wall. We continued to each room upstairs. The next room we stopped at was Todd's room. Claire went into the walk-in closet, continuing to burn the sage. She kneeled and waved the smoke in all corners. She then came back into the room.

We began to discuss the neighbors across the street. Todd said, "One time, I heard that house was cleansed due to all the activity, whatever cleansing means. I guess that's what we are doing here. I heard it was bad, and they ripped out the walls and rebuilt them. I was told that they used to hear people talking in a group. Supposedly, there used to be a women's sewing group that gathered in that house a long time ago. The house is really old."

I asked him, "How old are the people that live in the house now?"

He said, "Nine and twenty-one, all young."

I said, "I was just wondering because I remember when my wife and I came on Monday. We heard loud music playing that sounded like the big band era?"

Todd said, "Yeah."

I explained to the rest in the room that when we pulled into the driveway my wife said, "Listen. Don't you hear that music?"

I didn't hear any music.

"Tami told me it's coming from the direction of that house as she pointed to the house across the street and the one we are currently discussing. I got out of the truck and listened, and it is then that I did begin to hear the music and it did sound like very old music. My wife said, 'That is strange to hear that style of music today.' Next, Todd came out the front door and I told him we just heard what sounded like big band music coming from that house as I pointed across the street. I asked Todd if that was something they would play. He said, no. I thought, well, that was odd. Right after Todd walked outside, we didn't hear the music any longer."

After I finished the story, Claire said, "That is weird."

I said, "Yeah, that's why I asked the ages of the people there. It doesn't really matter, I guess, because even people that are old know that type of music is even older and they wouldn't be listening to that anyway."

We now walked across the hall to the bathroom, and she saged that room. She walked around and waved the burning sage into all areas of the room. Next, we began to head down the stairs which were directly outside this room. Right when Claire took her first step on the stairs, Tina asked her, "Why does the activity seem to only happen around me and not my dad?"

Claire told her, "It is your energy, and that is why they are attracted to you. Just know that they are not going to hurt you. They just want to play. You can tell them to leave. If it's making you feel scared, uneasy, or weird, just say, you must go. I don't want you here. Say, I hear you. A lot of times that is all they want is your attention."

Everyone now came down the steps and headed out back to the garage.

Todd and his dad built what they call the apartment above the garage. It's small, similar to a ranch home. There are two entrances to the apartment. One entrance steps into the garage that leads into the one bedroom while the other is by walking up the hill on a ramp that leads to the front of the house and into the front door. The front of the apartment faces the woods in the back of the property. We decided to walk up the steps into the garage and enter the one bedroom. It had furniture in it, but wasn't set up like a bedroom. Items such as an old wooden chest, headboard to a bed, boxes, etc. were just being stored in this room. Claire right away was drawn to the wooden chest that was against the far wall and behind the boxes which were stored and piled up in the center of the room. She asked, "Does this chest belong to Mary?" The Mary she was referring to was Mary Lou's stepmother.

Todd said, "Yes, it was hers."

As we walked from this room to the doorway to the living room/ kitchen area, Claire stopped and was looking at the knickknacks on a small shelf that was on the wall. She said, "Two pieces, I believe, were from the same Mary."

Todd said, "That is possible, but I will have to ask my mom to make sure."

We walked through the doorway and into the kitchen. Claire walked around, continuing to sage all areas of the kitchen and also the side room in the kitchen, which was a small bathroom. As she came out of that room, I asked her if she picked up on any name other than the name Paul in the house, maybe even a nickname.

She stopped, looked at me, and asked, "Does it start with a B?"

Steve and I just looked at each other and laughed.

I said, "It does start with a B."

Claire said, "I can't hear it clearly, but it sounds like a B."

Steve laughed and said, "If you would have gotten that name, I would've walked out of here!"

We all laughed.

Claire said, "It doesn't feel like it's from anyone in the house now, but from before. I am hearing like a radio tuning in, and I can't hear it clearly. I am mostly picking up on Mary's energy up here."

After we entered the living room, Todd said he wanted his sister here because she is twelve years older and may remember more things, but she recently had an operation and couldn't make it. Claire asked, "Does your sister believe in this kind of stuff?"

Todd said, "I think so, but she is more religious than I am."

Claire said, "That may bite you though."

Todd gave her a confused look and asked, "What do you mean bite?"

She said, "Many times people who are more religious have a hard time believing in the spirit world."

Todd said, "My dad built our house, this place, and the house beside us. I can remember when I was little that my sister would always say she would see a white dog over there at her house."

Claire asked, "Did they have a white dog?"

Todd asked, "Who?"

She said, "Your dad."

Todd said, "No, not that I know of."

I knew I had to remember to ask Mary Lou when we got back down to the house about the figurines and if they had a white dog. I said, "Maybe we should head back because I'm sure your mom is wondering where we are."

We went out the back door onto the porch.

The view is of a big yard that is on a hill and beyond the yard are woods.

Todd told us his mom would like to sit out here and watch the deer that would come out of the woods and into the yard. We walked along the path off the porch and around to the main house.

We went back into the living room as Mary Lou came out of her room to meet us. I asked her if her stepmom, Mary, gave her a figurine which was on the shelf in her apartment. She didn't hear me, so Todd, being right beside her, asked her. Todd said he would go back up and get it, so she could look at it. Todd headed back to the garage.

Claire asked Mary Lou, "Did your husband have a white dog at one time?"

Mary Lou said, "Yeah, his name was Whitey."

Claire and I looked at each other and laughed, thinking, who would have guessed a white dog named Whitey?

Claire told Mary Lou that her husband had the dog with him. Mary Lou's eyes lit up. She began to rub her hands and said, "That's great. Boy, what else do you have to tell me?"

We all got a kick out of that and laughed. Claire told her, "Your husband showed me a wedding picture of you two, and he said, 'Aren't I handsome?'"

Mary Lou had a big smile and said, "Yes."

Claire said, "Yes he was, and you looked beautiful."

This seemed to make Mary Lou's day.

Mary Lou told her, "I do have one question. Did anyone tell you when my time was up? I am the oldest and the last one living and wonder, why?"

Claire shook her head no and said, "They did say that you belong here in this house and not up there in the apartment. I'm told you are going to fall if you go back up there."

Mary Lou said, "Well, okay then. I guess I must stay here then."

Todd walked in with the figurine, and Mary Lou validated that her stepmom did give her that and the girl figurine next to it. Mary Lou started to show Claire all the pictures on the wall of her family and explained who they all were. We packed our equipment up as the two talked. It made me smile seeing Mary Lou so happy to talk about her family. I told Mary Lou that we would get her a copy of the walkthrough, so she could see and hear everything that she missed.

We did our investigation a few days ago on Monday, and now we finished the walkthrough. During this time, many things were validated between Claire and I with what we had seen, what we captured, and what she felt during her walkthrough. Even though this happened and we answered many questions, I left there feeling something was amiss. It kept bugging me that we missed a major piece even though the puzzle was coming together. Soon my feelings would be validated.

Chapter 5

Can't Shake This Feeling

The next day I talked to Todd. I told him that I would try and finish the video as soon as I could, so his mom could see and hear everything that she missed. I told him I was having trouble with my computer. He said that it was not a big deal. I thought otherwise. I couldn't shake the feeling of something missing and that I had to get it done for Mary Lou and get it done soon.

After a few days passed and my computer not cooperating, I told Todd I would just bring my laptop over and play each file of the walkthrough footage, so his mom could see it. I continued to feel like something was missing.

I said to Todd, "I don't know how to say this since it is your mom, but has she gone to the doctor recently for a checkup?"

He looked at me puzzled and asked, "Why?"

I said, "Since we left your house, I keep feeling something is going on with your mom. I can't pinpoint it, but I know something is missing. Again, it's your mom, and I don't know how to say this, but has she seen a doctor lately?"

Todd said, "I am always taking her to the doctors for checkups. They never find anything wrong."

I said, "Okay, I was just wondering if she had blood work and things like that done."

Todd said, "Yeah and everything comes back okay."

I heard what Todd said, but after the conversation, I kept thinking there might be something they were missing. I contacted Claire to see if she felt or heard anything from Spirit regarding Mary Lou getting hurt other than her falling. She told me she only got that she needed to be careful because of falling.

A few days later, Todd told me that something strange happened at the house. He described how his mom was sleeping and was woken up by the dog barking frantically. He said his mom got out of bed to see why the dog was barking, and when she opened her bedroom door, she noticed the front door wide open. The door was not only open, but the dead bolt was out as if still locked. She looked to her left and saw her brother, Bobby, sitting on the sofa, staring at her. Remember, Mary Lou is the last one of her siblings still alive. After Mary Lou and Bobby looked at each other, he faded away. I was so amazed at this story. It hit me at this moment that where Mary Lou saw Bobby was the same spot my ear rang loudly when Todd was showing me the pictures on the wall during my initial investigation. I kept replaying all these paranormal events through my head. I couldn't stop thinking about them and wondering how they all tied together.

A day or two later, I stopped over at Todd's to give his mom a gift. She wasn't home that day, but Todd said he would be sure to give it to her. I asked Todd to tell me again about the front door opening and how it looked. We went over to the door and he recreated what happened. This was one of many events that happened in this house regarding Spirit. What was Mary Lou's brother trying to tell her by opening the door?

Todd said, "While you are here, I want to show you something." Todd led me through the kitchen then outside to the back of the garage.

He said, "When you mentioned the vision of the lightning, it didn't make sense to me until yesterday. It hit me!"

Todd then pointed up and behind the property.

Behind the garage, the property goes up on a hill then levels off with woods for a few acres.

Todd said, "Do you see that tree?" He pointed to a tree that was directly in the middle behind the property and at the top of the hill.

He said, "The one that looks black."

I looked and saw the tree he was talking about, but there wasn't much of it left. It looked mostly dead.

From the base up until it stops, this tree is maybe six feet tall. That is all that was left of it.

Todd asked, "Do you know why it's mostly black?" I looked at him and he said, "Yeah, it's because it was hit by lightning numerous times!"

I said, "Are you freaking kidding me? Holy shit!" That explained why it was dying or pretty much dead too.

Todd said, "I never thought about it when you mentioned lightning and Claire mentioned the hanging."

This was another amazing example of how it all eventually comes together. I told Todd, "That has to be the tree Claire described and what I had seen. It definitely fits."

Todd said, "Yeah it probably is because that tree, at one time, was a lot larger and full, but that's what's left after the lightning strikes." Todd went on to describe that that wasn't the only tree on the property that got hit by lightning. He took me to the front corner of his house. He said, "This tree right here was struck by lightning too." The tree he showed me was right at the corner of the house. It was so close, the branches were almost touching the roof.

I felt it was really strange to have so many lightning strikes on this property. Even though he showed me two trees, I felt the one on the hill had to be the one in the vision. I was really glad Todd could validate the lightning I saw in that vision. This went a long way with helping me trust in everything I received from the other side.

Chapter 6

Flashes of Light

About a week after the walkthrough, I went over to meet Todd and Mary Lou at their house. I had my laptop and the video files on a flash drive, so Mary Lou could view them. Mary Lou was in her room when I arrived. She came out to greet me, and when she did, I asked her how she was and if anything new happened.

Mary Lou said, "I keep seeing flashes of light in the corner of my room."

I wondered where and asked her to show me. She took me in her room and said, "When I'm lying in bed, I see these flashes of light in the left corner over there."

I asked her, "Does anything else happen when you see this flash of light?"

She said, "No, just the flashes of light. I am getting woken up by a male voice telling me to get up. I'm tired and I want to sleep.

He lifts my arm and tells me I have to get up, but I say no." As she said, no, she swung her arm in a motion as if to get away and stop bugging her.

I laughed and said, "Yeah, you just want your sleep, right?"

She laughed and said, "Yeah."

We then went into the kitchen and sat down at the table. I opened the laptop, put in the flash drive, and brought up the first video file. I told Mary Lou I would play one file at a time. When one ends, I'd have to click on the next one for her to see. Mary Lou watched every second of each file very focused. To me, it seemed she wanted to hear every single word that was said. When we finally got to the footage of her apartment above the garage, she seemed even more interested. When Claire began to discuss her husband, she sat up, leaned in toward the laptop and had a big smile on her face. As Claire spoke of him, Mary Lou began to rub both her arms with her hands, continuing to keep the big smile. The love she had for her late husband really showed at that moment, and it made me feel really good to be able to share that with her. It was definitely a special moment.

I sat with Mary Lou until she viewed all the footage which was just under two hours in length. Afterward, Mary Lou told me to hold on. She had something she wanted to give me. After a few minutes, she came walking back in with a white garbage bag. She opened it and began to pull out things she crocheted. The bag was filled with them. She told me to pick out a few more and give them to my wife.

I said, "It might make her cry."

She said, "Tell her if she cries when you give them to her, I want them back."

I said, "Okay, I will tell her that." We all laughed.

Mary Lou said, "I like you. You need to come back more often."

On the drive home, I kept thinking about what Mary Lou said about the flashes she was seeing and the man telling her to get up. Why was he telling her to get up? Why was she seeing flashes? Why did the door open? It was frustrating to feel there was something missing even more now and not being able to figure it out, not knowing why this was happening. I knew it wasn't good, but I just couldn't put this piece of the puzzle together. It was really frustrating to not get these answers. In one way, I strongly felt something was going to happen to Mary Lou, and a part of me was second-guessing myself, thinking I was looking into it too much and I was wrong. That battle was real between the logical mind and the spiritual side. Since this happened, I had learned to trust my feelings, but at that time I was still second-guessing myself.

When I arrived home, I texted Claire to tell her about all of this and get her opinion. As I waited for her reply, I was hoping it was a good sign, but deep down, I knew she would tell me something I didn't want to hear. Soon, my text tone sounded on my phone and it was her replying. She said the flashes to her feel angelic. The angels were with her. She didn't give me an answer on why the guy was telling her to get up other than it was family. Claire said there were quite a few family members visiting her.

Chapter 7

Say It Isn't So

The next day, I told Todd what Claire said regarding the flashes being angelic.

I told Todd, "I think your mom is great, and I get a kick out of her. With what she is seeing and hearing, plus my constant feeling of something missing regarding her, is driving me nuts trying to understand the whys."

Claire mentioned before that Mary Lou had to be careful not to fall, but it felt like more than that to me. I told him, "I am glad your mom got to see the walkthrough, and please tell her that my wife loved her gifts. Thank your mom from my wife." I mentioned again, "I know it's your mom, and I don't know how to say it other than to watch her to make sure she is okay." I couldn't get the urgency out of my head.

The next day, Todd did not come to work. After I got home, a voice told me to call Todd. The phone rang, and as soon as it stopped, I heard Todd say, "Well, you were right, Jeff." There was a sense of worry in his voice.

I asked, "Right? Right about what?"

Todd said, "They just took my mom away in the ambulance."

I said, "Oh my God, is she alright? What happened?"

Todd said, "I stayed home from work because I felt sick. I woke up, and when I came downstairs, I looked in my mom's room and she looked asleep. I went back to bed because I felt so bad. When I awoke again, I came downstairs to see what she was doing. I noticed she was still in her room in her bed. I walked over to her and I felt something was wrong because she doesn't usually sleep this long. She sat up and I noticed right away her face was not normal. She looked like she had a stroke."

I told Todd how sorry I was and that I hoped she would be alright. He told me he would keep me updated.

Chapter 8

She Can Hear You

Todd informed me the next day that our local hospital had to fly his mom to Hershey Medical Center because they were more capable of treating her. I really began to question why Spirit was not more specific on the messages to me or to Claire? Why was it always a puzzle to put together?

Mary Lou ended up staying in Hershey for a few days with no significant improvement. Todd told me that they could do nothing more for her and that he had to decide where she was to go—either back home or to a nursing type facility. The hospital said that she would never improve from the state that she was in. In addition to this, Mary Lou had in her will that if she became in this type of state that she wanted to basically not be helped and to let her die. Mary Lou had what was called a DNR, which means do not resuscitate—no medical intervention and no tube feeding. After I heard this news, I felt really bad that I did not see this coming. Thinking about it and how concerned I was toward something happening to Mary Lou, I couldn't believe I didn't put the pieces of the puzzle together fast enough. It was all I could think of. In my opinion, at this time, I felt let down by Spirit. I felt if I didn't get specifics, why didn't Claire? I did not understand why the message did not come. Why show and tell us so much, but not be specific about this detail? This would be all I could think about for the next week.

Todd informed me that he made his decision, and he decided to let them take his mom to a nursing home. Honestly, I was hoping he decided to let her come back home for what looked like her last days. I understood Todd's reasoning for deciding on the nursing home. He said he didn't want Tina, who is only ten years old, to see her grandmother like this at home and possibly witness her dying. He also said, "I just don't have the time to take care of her. It will be a full-time job looking after her, and the nursing home has qualified people to do that."

I told him I understood his concerns and that he needed to do what was best for him and his daughter. His mom would understand.

Mary Lou was transferred to a local nursing home. I told Todd that I would like to go see her, but wanted to wait a few days, so the family could be there with her. Todd kept me updated each day on how his mom was doing. When things like this happen, you always hope in the back of your mind that there's a possibility that it isn't as bad as originally thought and the person might improve, just a glimmer of hope, but this wasn't the case. Each day, Todd would tell me that there was no improvement, that the doctors said that the state she was in, she would never improve from this point on. He said the doctors told him that she had no reaction, and that she did not hear or recognize anyone. I told Todd not to listen to any of that. I said the doctors do not know everything. I told him to go in there and talk to her, tell her whatever he felt he needed to tell her. I told him that she would hear him and know it was him. Todd said, okay, and that he would do just that. The next day, Todd told me that he spoke to his mom and told her what he wanted to say. He said she just stared, and it didn't seem like she was reacting to anything. I told him I felt without a doubt that she heard everything and understood what he said to her.

Chapter 9

Believe

A few days passed, and I asked Todd if it was alright if I went in to see Mary Lou at the nursing home? Todd said, sure, that would be fine.

My wife and I arrived, walked in, and were pointed in the right direction from the main desk. As we walked through the halls, many patients were lying on a gurney or sitting in a chair covered with a blanket and looked sick. Most had their heads back with their mouths wide open. It honestly creeped me out. Others were sitting in chairs around the nurses' station with an agitated look on their faces. My wife asked me, "Do you know why they are sitting around the nurses' desk like that?"

I said, "I have no clue."

She said, "They are on a time-out. They didn't behave and they are now on a time-out."

I found this kind of comical. It was like preschool, but with the elderly. We walked by all the grouchy looking ones on time-outs as we arrived at Mary Lou's room. After seeing her at home, laughing with her just a week prior, to now see her lying in bed, frail, her mouth wide open, and her eyes fixed on the wall at the foot of her bed, was a sad sight to see. Todd's sister was the only one in the room with Mary Lou. She was sitting beside the bed and holding her mom's hand. As my wife and Todd's sister were discussing Mary Lou's condition, I kept watching Mary Lou's eyes as people walked by her room. Her bed was close to the door, and if you were lying in the bed, the door would be to your left from the foot of the bed. As someone would walk by, I would see her eyes follow them. Every time someone would walk by the open door, she did this.

Todd's sister said she would be right back, that she would leave us with her mom. I walked over to Mary Lou's left side and leaned over to her. She turned her head toward me and lifted her hand to me, so I held her hand. I could feel her grip tightening as she stared at me. She looked right into my eyes and I said, "Hi, Mary Lou. Tami and I wanted to come see you." Even though Mary Lou's mouth was crooked and open from the stroke, her mouth raised a little as I spoke to her.

Tami said, "Jeff, did you see that? I honestly think she just smiled at you."

I nodded my head and kept eye contact with Mary Lou while I held her hand.

I said, "Mary Lou, it will be okay. It will all be okay."

Mary Lou might not have been able to talk, but I could tell by her eyes that she knew me and understood what I just said to her. I just knew it. All I could do was hold her hand while looking into her eyes and telling her everything would be okay. It was a moment I would never forget.

Mary Lou passed away on April 30, 2018. It was within days of Tami and I visiting her. She asked many times when we were at her house, why was she the only one left? Why, out of all her family, was she the only one left? She wanted to go and be with them.

Chapter 10

Letting Go

Over the coming weeks and months, Todd would tell me of activity in their home and the apartment above the garage. While things seemed to settle down with certain activities, things seemed to pick up regarding other activities. The spirit of the children seemed to take over from the family of Mary Lou. The children who Claire and I saw and described made themselves known to the daughter of the family that moved into the apartment above the garage. The daughter said she saw them. She heard them laughing and playing. She described it as she felt they were playing hide and seek. This stuck out because that was exactly what Claire said just weeks earlier during her walkthrough. It seemed most of the activity surrounding Mary Lou was her family that passed before her warning her to get up. Her arm was pulled while she was in bed, and she was told to get up. The front door opened and, again, she was told to get out of bed. She was being protected from hurting herself when she felt someone grab her waist and guide her back to bed on one occasion. Why would the spirits guide her back to bed one time and then tell her to get up and open the front door another? After all this, she then witnessed the bright light in the corner of her room. Were these her angels preparing her? We received so many answers, but we were also left with so many questions.

As time passed, I got to play everything over and over again in my mind. What if I would have been told by Spirit that Mary Lou was going to have a stroke? Would Todd have believed me? Would he have taken her to the hospital? If he had, how could she possibly be diagnosed without symptoms? Many scenarios played out in my head. I felt for certain that Mary Lou's family were the ones that kept visiting her, first trying to warn her, and then they came to protect her. Now we know those family members, along with her angels, were there to guide her home. While I was very confused, and at one point mad at Spirit for not letting us know what was going to happen, I have come to the understanding that I need to have faith that what happened was supposed to happen the way it did. At the time, it did. The validation I received from Spirit and the understanding of faith ended up being an experience that I would never forget. From this point on, I stopped second-guessing myself.

I have faith that there is a plan and that everything happens for a reason.

Conclusion

A few years have now gone by since this experience and the passing of Mary Lou. Todd told me that since his mom passed, all activity stopped. The only thing that happened was when the children were heard and seen in the apartment above the garage afterward, but then it all slowly went away.

There will always be skeptics no matter what evidence is presented. These skeptics will always find another explanation as to why these experiences are everything but paranormal.

This story happened exactly how it is written. I spent many hours researching, but couldn't find documented evidence of any hanging that took place or of any meeting house, hotel, or gathering place on this property. I did learn of a wagon shop nearby, but not directly where this home now stands. The further back the research goes in time, the harder it is to validate events, especially a hanging. The only clear audio capture we received was the name Baby Doll. This has yet to be validated, but that is clearly the message given. The proof came from the energy of the home and property. This energy was felt through the personal feelings/experiences of each person involved in this story. Validation came from how Spirit worked through my visions and through Claire to show who was still part of the property from long ago. It also shows how family and other loved ones stay with us after they pass on.

This is a story to me, and hopefully for you, that shows love never dies. We are never alone because our passed loved ones are always with us, protecting us, and guiding us. Angels are real, and we need not fear anything regarding death because we live on. When the time comes, we all will be guided home to meet our loved ones again.

After Thoughts

So many things intrigued me in just the few weeks I was involved with this home. One story that I kept replaying in my head was the neighbor who was rumored to be a "Witch." I couldn't stop thinking about this woman's ashes being placed in a can then buried in the yard under a tree. How can one person be so disrespected not once, but twice? How bad would a person have to be in life to just put her in a produce can and believe this was okay? It made me want to find out more about this woman and her personality. I also kept thinking of the can randomly thrown in the woods behind the garage.

On April 11, 2022, my curiosity got the best of me, and after contacting Todd, I drove to his home. Todd and I went to the area of the woods where he believes his dad threw the can containing the witch's ashes.

The property behind the garage is on a steep hill. Once we reached the edge of the woods, Todd said, "If I remember the story correctly, we need to go left and up." We zigzagged through the brush and came upon a slightly flat area.

Todd said, "I believe this is the area." I looked around, trying to get a feel of the area and to see if I was drawn to where this can was thrown. About forty yards above us, there was a ridge that ran left to right.

Ridge bordering property line.

Todd pointed and said, "That is our property line. Beyond that ridge is not our property, so I believe the area where we are standing is where the can would be. That's even if we can find it. Remember, this happened way back in the early '70s or before."

I said, "Yeah, I didn't expect to find it. I wanted to get a feel of the area and just look around. I had to walk up here. I'd like to get a metal detector and see if it could locate the can."

Todd said, "I don't have a problem with that. Sure, do whatever you want."

As we stood there, my eyes kept getting drawn to two areas. One was a tree that really stood out from all the others. It was a skinny, but very tall tree with roots wrapping around the base and continuing to the top of the tree. A few feet from the base, there were two knots or openings that looked like eyes. The other spot I was drawn to was a few feet to the left of that tree. I was drawn to this long, large flat rock. It was on its side, leaning up against three even skinnier trees. This rock reminded me of an old-style tombstone.

Tree with roots wrapped around it.

*Image of rock in woods that reminded
me of a tombstone on its side.*

I thanked Todd for taking me to the area to look around. I was glad to finally get the opportunity. My next step was to get a metal detector to see if the areas I was drawn to would be the correct one. Until that was an option, I wanted to send the photos I took to Dana, a gifted friend of mine, to see if she felt anything by looking at them. I sent the photos with no explanation at all, just a few photos of the area where Todd and I were standing. After texting the photographs to her, she replied within a few minutes. Her response was very impressive.

Her text read:

Wandering, gray, I'm getting a rush of air, rustling wisps, something that looks like a figure. Long hair. I want to say female. Whispering. I can't tell if something is supposed to be here or not supposed to be here. I keep hearing something muffled. The whispering I heard sounded like a little girl, but had an air of maturity to it, if that makes sense? I saw a little girl in a gray dress and bonnet. I thought I got children.

I stood looking at my phone thinking, *wow, what a great read, especially since she just looked at the photos.* From the time I sent them to when she responded was only a minute or two. I was amazed at her accuracy. By her reading of the photos, it felt to me that she was picking up on the witch and also the children that are part of this story—one girl in particular. When she responded with gray dress, I immediately thought of my vision where I saw three kids in nightshirts. The only difference was none of the kids I saw had a bonnet on.

I originally sent Dana eight photos of the area of the woods Todd and I were standing in. Out of those eight photos, Dana saw the girl in the gray dress giggling by the same tree I was originally drawn to—the one with the roots wrapping around it. Again, I was amazed by this.

Saturday May 14, 2022, I finally had the opportunity to rent a metal detector and go back into the woods above Todd's house. I knew it was a long shot that the metal detector would locate the can, but I had to at least try.

With the metal detector and a shovel in hand, my wife and I

walked up the hill behind Todd's house. As we reached the edge of the yard and where the woods met, I noticed how high the weeds happened to be. Four weeks ago when I came to the same area with Todd, it was easy access to the area, but now it was overgrown with weeds and grass. I figured it would grow a little bit, but I stood there in disbelief how overgrown it was. I couldn't find where the path was or the specific area I was at just a few weeks ago.

I told Tami, "Well, we are here now, so if you don't want to continue I understand, but I have to try."

Tami, as always, said, "No, it's fine. I'm coming with you."

We both zigzagged through the brush, trying to make our way to the flat area where I stood with Todd. Not only was it overgrown, but the bugs swirling around our faces were really bad this time.

I looked around and said, as I was waving my hand back and forth, trying to keep those annoying bugs away from my face, "It has to be somewhere on this side. I just can't tell from all these high weeds."

Tami followed as I kept going up and to the left. I looked to my left, and I saw the tree with the roots wrapping around it, so I turned and pointed as I told Tami, "This is it. I wasn't sure at first that we were going to find it."

Tree with roots wrapped around it.
Notice the overgrowth of weeds in this
image compared to my first visit.

We walked to the tree that had the roots wrapped around it. Tami turned on the metal detector and waved it right to left around the perimeter of the tree. The alarm sounded. The screen then showed what was detected. The word *iron* was highlighted, and it read the object detected was four inches down. I grabbed the shovel and began to dig. As soon as I stuck the shovel into the dirt, it hit a rock. As I dug, more pieces of rock appeared.

I said to Tami, "I am guessing the iron detected may be from all the rocks because there is nothing here but shale."

Tami waved the detector over the hole and no alarm sounded

this time. She waved it back over the rocks I dug up and it alarmed again.

Image of metal detector and shale.

We walked to the left slightly in hopes we could locate the can and maybe the remains. As soon as we did, we heard rustling to our left up in a tree. We looked and saw two huge turkey vultures landing in a tree and resting. Just as we began to walk toward that area, the skies opened up and it began to rain.

I looked at Tami and then to the sky and said, "You got to be kidding me!"

There was no rain in the forecast until later in the day. We were in the woods for a matter of ten minutes and it decided to rain.

I looked at Tami and she was just laughing and saying, "Oh well. It's only rain."

I said, "We better head back quick! The rain is coming down stronger!"

We zigzagged our way back down the hill as the rain turned into a downpour. We reached the car, and we both were soaked. I opened the back door, threw in the metal detector, and then quickly got into the driver's seat as Tami got into the passenger seat. Tami and I looked at each other in disbelief, disbelief it rained at that exact time and disbelief as soon as we sat in the car, the rain stopped. I looked up through the droplets in the windshield and to the sky above the woods and it was clear and sunny.

I looked at Tami and said, "What the hell? It stopped raining. Either someone didn't want us there, or it just happened to pour hours earlier than forecasted and at the same time we arrived at that spot in the woods. Is this odd or what?"

Tami looked at me and said, "Yes, that was definitely odd."

We decided to leave and head home. I knew locating the can was a long shot to begin with, but I wanted to try. Now with nature taking over with so much overgrowth, we both felt the odds were not in our favor.

After we arrived home, I sent a few photos of the woods to Dana just as I did before. I explained to her how I waited too long to return because the weeds were so high now.

After looking at the photos, Dana texted me the following:

I got the girl in the bonnet again. There was someone peeking out. Possibly a child. A boy. Heard a giggle. I just heard, 'Doesn't want to be found.' It was a whisper like a child's. Did you get anything while you were there?

Kidding, I replied:

All I got were ticks and bugs.

I told her how it poured soon after we stepped into the woods. The rain wasn't supposed to start until later in the day. It stopped as soon as we returned to the car.

Dana's next text read:

Well, that's an interesting coincidence. Funny how that works with us.

I found myself questioning many things regarding the witch story. Was this woman a witch? Did the husband of this supposed witch really cremate her and put her ashes in a can? Was the can holding her ashes just randomly thrown in the woods? Was this a story told just to mess with Todd's family since they didn't like the neighbor? Was it a story Todd's dad made up so his kids would stay out of the woods? Was this story misinterpreted over all these years?

Were the turkey vultures a sign?

Why did it rain only at that specific time in the woods and stop as soon as we returned to our car?

Did the children fade away as Todd believed, or were they still there?

By what Dana felt and saw, their presence continued.

It seemed to me whatever or whomever was in those woods, they wanted to be left alone.

My daughter, Lauren, has recently been living in the apartment above the garage where Mary Lou once lived. She told me she doesn't notice anything out of the ordinary except her cats seem to play and follow something that isn't there. Lauren jokes and says, "I tell people when it happens, the cats are just playing with their friends

One day, I stopped to visit Lauren. I saw Todd in his driveway as

I pulled in. As we were chatting, he said he found old family photos and that next time I come over I should stop in the house, so he could show them to me to see if anyone in the photos may be the guy I saw with the three kids in the vision I had. I told him I would stop over on Friday.

When I arrived that Friday, Todd had a box of photo albums and loose photos that were stacked in the box. He set the box on the kitchen table as we stood aside of it. As Todd was going through each page or stack of pictures, he handed me one and said, "Is this him?"

Each time I would say, "No, that's not him. His face was rounder."

I said to Todd, "The man I saw has the same features as the men in these photos, but none are the same guy. The ones that I picked out were all family of Mary Lou. Each time it was either her brother Bobby at different ages or her uncle Paul."

I said, "It must be someone on your mom's side since I keep picking out the same two guys. Whoever he is, he has the same features as the men on her side of the family."

We continued to go through the entire box of more than one hundred photos. As we got to the end, Todd handed me an old photo. There were a few people standing side by side. I looked at each face, and when I got to the last person on the left, I brought the photo closer, so I could try and see it clearer. I was shocked to finally see someone that resembled my vision of the older man.

Since the photo was taken at a slight distance and my eyes aren't like they used to be, Todd went and retrieved his magnifying glass, so I could see these guys' faces clearer. Todd returns with this big magnifying glass which had a light attached to it.

I said, "Guess your eyes are as good as mine, huh? Sucks getting old."

Todd nodded his head as we both laughed.

With the magnifying glass in one hand and the picture in the other, I focused on this one man's face. I was honestly in shock when the guy I only saw in a vision seemed to be staring back at me in an actual photograph taken long ago. Time kind of stood still at that moment.

The gentleman on the far left resembles the sketch of the man with the lantern.

I told him, "I can't say it with one hundred percent certainty, but it sure resembles him."

Todd told me to keep the few photographs that I felt looked like the man. He thought I could do some further research, and if I found someone, maybe the faces would match.

Todd said, "Let's go out front. You mentioned when you saw that guy and the kids that there were also steps in your vision. I think there may have been steps at one time."

I said, "Seriously? Are you kidding me?"

Todd said, "No follow me. I'll show you what I mean."

Todd led me out the front door and turned to the right on the porch. He walked across the yard and stopped where the driveway that goes to the garage out back and the yard meet. Facing the house, we stood to the far left of it.

Todd said, "There was a sidewalk here at one time. There might have been steps here at that time. When my parents bought the property, the land didn't look like it does now. Right past where we are standing, that hill was higher back then." Todd pointed to the ridge that surrounds his property. "My dad excavated this whole area prior to building the house."

I said, "So the end of the yard where we are standing was higher and possibly had steps at that time?"

Todd said, "Yes. I can't remember for sure, but for some reason I remember a sidewalk along here and then the steps would be here where we stand."

I always felt that my vision of the man and three kids was in the front yard at the edge where the yard and Shoemakersville Road meet, so I brought this to Todd's attention.

Todd said, "Well, you may be right. Show me where you mean."

I walked to approximately where the main driveway is and the road.

I said, "This is where I felt the steps were at one time."

I asked Todd, "You said the property was higher a long time ago, so would it possibly have been higher at the end of the yard where we stand, higher here than the road, which would mean someone would have to step up unto the yard from the road?"

Todd said, "That is possible since the yard would have been

higher at this area, and I am pretty sure there was a mailbox here at one time." Todd pointed to the side where I felt the steps were located. "That would make sense if the mailbox was at that spot, you would have to step up to get to the yard."

I said, "That makes sense. I don't know for certain it was at this spot. It just felt it was when I had the vision, but yes, I agree with what you said."

Seeing the photos and hearing about the steps really helped me in trying to validate some of the visions that I had. It is always welcomed anytime we as Mystics, Mediums, Psychics, etc. are validated.

While I had the time and opportunity, I wanted to ask Todd about another subject that had been on my mind.

I asked Todd, "Has anyone that lived in your house ever experienced or spoke of the paranormal prior to you asking me to visit initially? I know I asked you this question a few times. Every time you said that nothing like this happened prior to Tina and your mom experiencing the activity and you asking me to find the answers. *Even though this scenario was possible, I keep feeling there must be more.* When I first came here, you stated the activity just started happening, but since then, you told me a few stories that show there was prior activity. I also feel your parents may have been more open to the spirit world than you might know. Your dad seemed to have a strong intuition, and your mom had the ability to see spirits. I want to understand and get the story correct regarding when the activity first started. Was there any activity prior to you asking me to come over to help initially?"

Todd said, "Yeah, that was usually just with my dad."

I asked Todd, "You mean just since he passed? Nothing before that?"

Todd said, "Yes. Nothing before that."

Todd hesitated then said, "Well, when I was a kid, and it was hardly ever I would get an uneasy feeling when I was in the basement. Though after my dad died, the neighbor across the street would say that he at one time looked over and saw a male figure walking around over here, walking down the bank and toward the house and disappear. He knew it wasn't me because at the same time he saw the male, he saw me on the lawn tractor mowing the grass. It had to have been my dad. Also, shortly after my dad died, I could hear the steps creak like someone was coming upstairs, and I could smell his old leather work boots, but he never came around the corner. My bedroom at that time was at the top of the steps where the bathroom is now."

I said to Todd, "Just so I understand this correctly, there was no activity prior to your dad passing, then things happened here and there over the years, but then really picked up just prior to your mom passing?"

Todd said, "Yes, then as soon as she died, it was pretty much nothing. Only thing after that I can recall is the children that were seen in the apartment by the tenants at that time and that they said the kids' toys would turn on by themselves. Other than that, there is nothing."

I said, "I just feel there are more stories. Did your parents ever talk about the paranormal, or do you remember any stories from your siblings, neighbors, or anyone regarding this property? You and your family have been here for many years. The stories that I have been told make me feel like your parents especially were more open to the spirit world, but may have never talked about it. You lived on this property your whole life, so there is a lot of history on this property, and nobody experienced anything at all or talked about it until your dad passed. Then all of sudden, this hanged guy appears after possibly hundreds of years and your daughter sees it. There was nobody before?"

Todd said, "Nope. There was nothing."

I said, "That's crazy. I saw him in a vision. Claire saw him when she was here. Tina saw him in the basement. All three of us described the same guy. Why did he only show up at that moment in time? Somehow at some point, I would think he had to make himself known to someone. Even the kids that were seen by Tina, Claire, and me, they seem to still be on the property. Who are these kids and why did I see them with that older man? It just makes me wonder if there are other stories to be told that involve these spirits. The older man felt like family, but who were these three kids?"

I asked Todd, "When Claire was here, I don't remember her that day or anywhere on footage of that day that she tried crossing any of the spirits over that were here. So, if the kids are still connected to the property, why isn't this man that got hanged? Why would he just leave?"

Todd said, "I don't know. You know, I never thought of that. Tina would see him, and then after my mom died, nothing. Even when you guys were first here and got that 'Baby Doll' on audio, I didn't hear it. I went up the steps at that time."

I asked, "Did you ever ask Tina or any other family member if that name meant anything to them?"

Todd said, "Yes and nobody has ever heard or said that."

I said, "That 'baby doll' was so clear. Somebody was called Baby Doll. It had to have meant something. I knew the chances of me validating the hanged man and the baby doll audio capture was very unlikely."

I asked Todd again, "Have your parents ever talked to you about seeing, hearing, experiencing the paranormal in any way? Any stories at all?"

Todd said, "No, never. I do know the house my mom grew up in was haunted. It was in Boyertown. She was born in that house. You didn't want to be there at night. At night, you would not go into that attic. If you did, you would get what you needed and get out. My dad never said anything regarding that stuff."

Todd changed the subject and said, "I don't think you know this story. At one point before my dad died, my mom would get bad dreams. The one time she was having a bad dream. I woke up because I heard her. I was right across the hall in my room. The next day, I asked her if she had a bad dream last night. She said, 'Your father was at the bottom of the steps yelling my name.' She said she would be calling out for him, but he couldn't help, so she would ask her dad, who was dead, for help, and only then would the dreams stop."

Todd said, "For whatever reason, she was being tormented. You couldn't get actors to make noises like she was making."

I said, "You did tell me about her nightmares after your dad passed where she felt like she was floating. Those happened after your dad passed, but these you just told me happened prior to him passing, right?"

Todd said, "Yes, those other ones were after he died, but, yes, these I just said about happened before he died. It's hard to remember since he died in '92, but, seriously, now that I think about it, those dreams of her being tormented first started maybe a month before he passed."

I asked, "Afterward, did your mom ever wake up and say it bothered her or say these dreams scared her?"

Todd said, "No."

Todd said, "Well, actually, one time when Tina was little, I was installing spindles and a handrail on the basement stairs. I didn't want Tina to fall through. While I was doing that, I had my mom at the top holding it while I fastened it at the bottom. My mom said she saw my dad standing behind me watching me do it."

I said, "See, that's what I keep getting at. I keep asking about your parents' beliefs, abilities, and other paranormal stories, how your dad could mention someone and in five minutes, they would call, your mom seeing Spirit. There seems to be many stories that make me believe they both were more in tune with the spirit world."

It seemed the discussion I was having with Todd this day somehow jogged a few paranormal memories that were hidden.

Todd said, "After my dad passed, my mom would tell me while she lived in the apartment, a lot of times, my dad would be laying in the bed with her. He would get up, and he would tell her that he had to go to work. Then he would be gone."

I asked, "Was this in a dream, or did she see and feel it awake?"

Todd said, "No, it wasn't a dream. She saw and felt it."

I said, "Everything you told me and now telling me really leads me to believe your parents may have been more open to the spirit world than they let on to everyone."

I left Todd's today feeling happy that a few pieces fell into place, but I knew the chances of me validating the hanged man and the baby doll audio capture was very unlikely. It had to have meant something. Tina, Claire, and I all saw him at different times, and the audio capture was so clear. Those two pieces of the puzzle may not fit quite yet, but the puzzle as a whole has come together to make a clearer picture that shows this house and the spirit world had a connection.

This entire story will always stay with me. I find it randomly entering my thoughts. There are moments I get lost in my thoughts. I learned a lot about my gifts/abilities in those few weeks. At times, I'm frustrated and even angry at the other side, but in the end, I come away very humbled. Spirit has a way of doing that.

Todd, I knew for many years. In just a short few weeks, I got to know his mother whose spirit will always be with me. I feel very blessed for being given the opportunity to help his family.

I hope you enjoyed this story, one which had so many elements, but it is a story of family foremost, how the family connection and the love never fade away.

When I first met Mary Lou, she had a question that really bothered her as she asked...

"I don't know why I can't go to be with them, and I don't understand why I am the only one left?"

I could tell Mary Lou strongly felt and wanted to know, from deep within her, the answers to these questions.

May her soul now rest in peace.

Acknowledgements

Thank you to:

First and foremost, my family. I love you all very much. Family is everything to me.

Todd and Tina for welcoming me into your home, being open and trusting me to not only help, but to also tell this story.

Mary Lou it was a pleasure to get to know you, even though it was for only a short time. Your spirit will always live on.

Steve and Natalya Reber for your friendship and for joining me during this journey.

Nadine Witmer for your proofreading skills, your friendship and your constant support.

Dana Marie Vollmer for your friendship and your incredible insight into the spirit world.

Michael Adams for helping me with the research.

Leesport Historical Society.

James Freeman for taking the time to discuss the history of the area.

Richard Strause and Elaine Strause for welcoming me into the

Historical Society, answering my research questions and giving me a tour. Your passion for history is evident.

Gary E. Phillips for your book, Running Waters, The History of the City of Reading's Water Supply.

Blue Sky Design for the perfect cover design.

This story could not be told without each of you. Thank you all.

www.ingramcontent.com/pod-product-compliance
Lightning Source LLC
Chambersburg PA
CBHW051226160726
47994CB00002B/766